My World

Editor: Katie Puckett
Designer: John Jamieson
Managing Editor: Miranda Smith

Activity illustrations: Gina Suter
Additional design: Joanne Brown
DTP co-ordinator: Nicky Studdart
Production controller: Kelly Johnson
Artwork archivists: Wendy Allison, Steve Robinson
Indexer: Sue Lightfoot

KINGFISHER
Kingfisher Publications Plc
New Penderel House
283–288 High Holborn
London WC1V 7HZ

First published by Kingfisher Publications Plc 1999
ISBN 0 7534 0375 7

This edition published for The Book People Ltd,
Hall Wood Avenue, Haydock, St Helens WA11 9UL
ISBN 1 85613 557 8

1BP / 0599 / H&Y / HBM(HBM) / 128IMA

A CIP catalogue record for this book is available from the British Library.

Printed in Hong Kong

My World

TED SMART

Contents

About this book

My World is full of information about the world in which we live. You can find out all about animals and plants, people and places, transport, outer space and how things work.

Some pages have a special activity box. There are lots of things to make, games to play, puzzles to solve and experiments to try. The index at the back of the book will help you to find information quickly.

Angela Wilkes

ACTIVITY BOX

The Universe

The Universe

Everything that exists is part of the Universe. The Earth is in the Universe and so are the Sun, the Moon and everything else in space. The Universe is enormous. No one knows how big it is, or where it begins and ends.

Some red giants grow into huge supergiants.

The Universe is made up of billions of stars. Stars are huge balls of burning gases. New stars are born all the time, from clouds of dust and gas. Old stars fade and grow cold.

A star shines for billions of years.

Then it swells up into a big star called a red giant.

The outer layers of the star may escape into space.

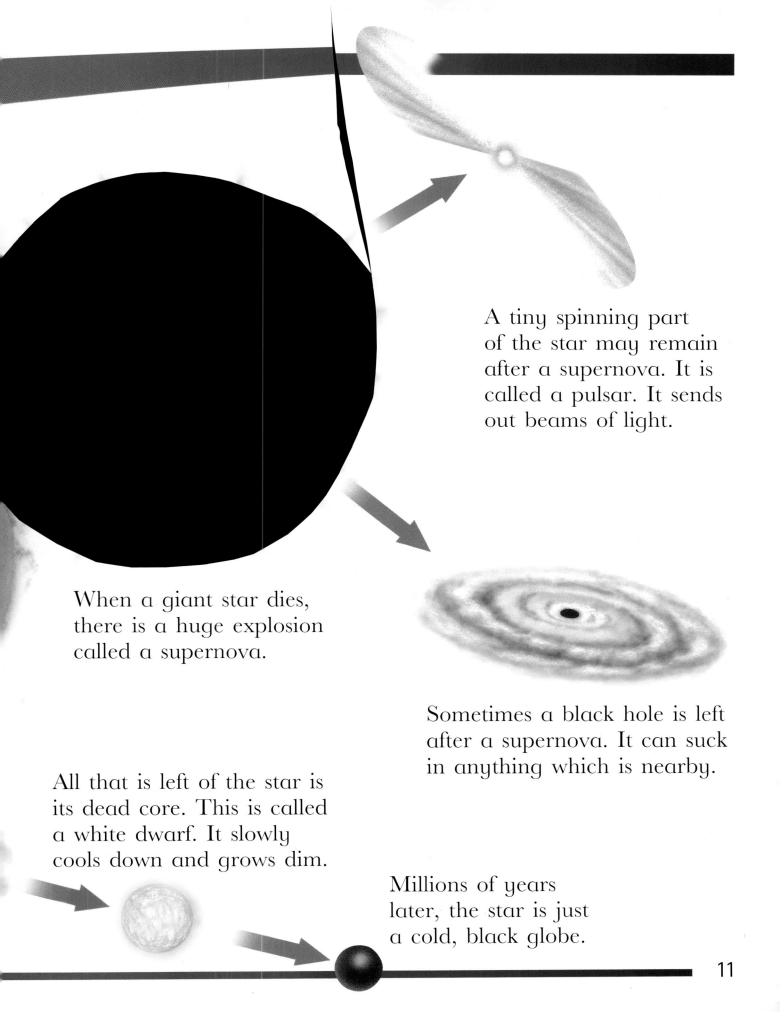

A tiny spinning part of the star may remain after a supernova. It is called a pulsar. It sends out beams of light.

When a giant star dies, there is a huge explosion called a supernova.

Sometimes a black hole is left after a supernova. It can suck in anything which is nearby.

All that is left of the star is its dead core. This is called a white dwarf. It slowly cools down and grows dim.

Millions of years later, the star is just a cold, black globe.

Night sky

On a clear night you can see that the sky is full of stars. Many of them form patterns in the sky, called constellations. Long ago, people gave constellations names to make it easier to recognize them.

People in the northern part of the world see the stars shown here in the night sky.

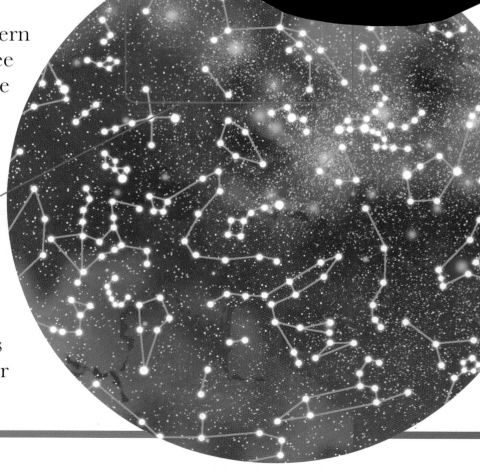

This constellation is called Pegasus, after a mythical horse.

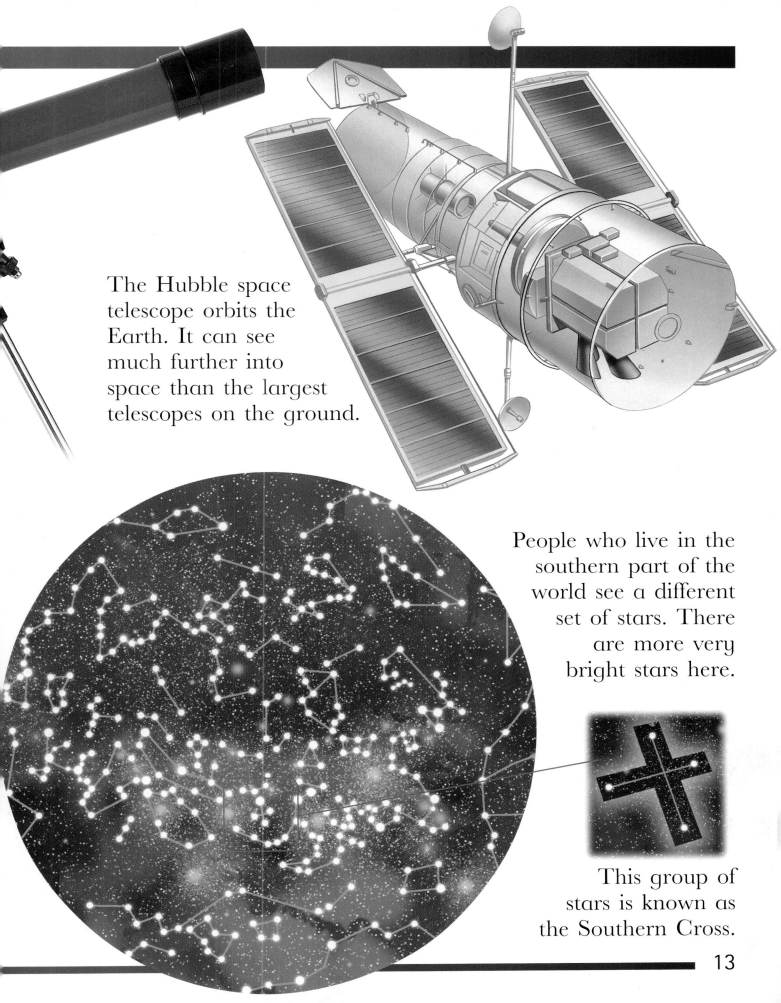

The Hubble space telescope orbits the Earth. It can see much further into space than the largest telescopes on the ground.

People who live in the southern part of the world see a different set of stars. There are more very bright stars here.

This group of stars is known as the Southern Cross.

Galaxies

The Universe is made of gigantic groups of stars called galaxies. There are billions of stars in each galaxy. Planet Earth and the Sun are near the edge of a galaxy called the Milky Way.

If you look at the sky on a clear night, you may see a faint band of stars. This is part of the Milky Way. Our galaxy is a giant spiral of stars, slowly turning around a large group of stars in the middle.

The central part of a galaxy is called the nucleus.

Draw a spiral galaxy in glue on a big piece of black card. Sprinkle glitter over the glue. Tip the card up to shake off any loose glitter. Wait for the glue to dry, then hang it on your wall.

New stars form from areas of gas and dust.

Galaxies are different shapes and sizes. These are the three main types.

Irregular-shaped galaxy

Egg-shaped galaxy

Spiral galaxy

The Solar System

A family of planets, moons, comets and other chunks of rock is constantly spinning around the Sun. This family is called the Solar System. There are nine planets in our Solar System. They are made of rocks, liquids, metal or gas.

The planets in the Solar System are millions of kilometres apart. They are very different from one another. Mercury is the closest planet to the Sun, and Pluto is the furthest away. Jupiter is the largest planet. It is so big that all the other planets could fit inside it.

Jupiter

Mercury

Venus

Earth

Mars

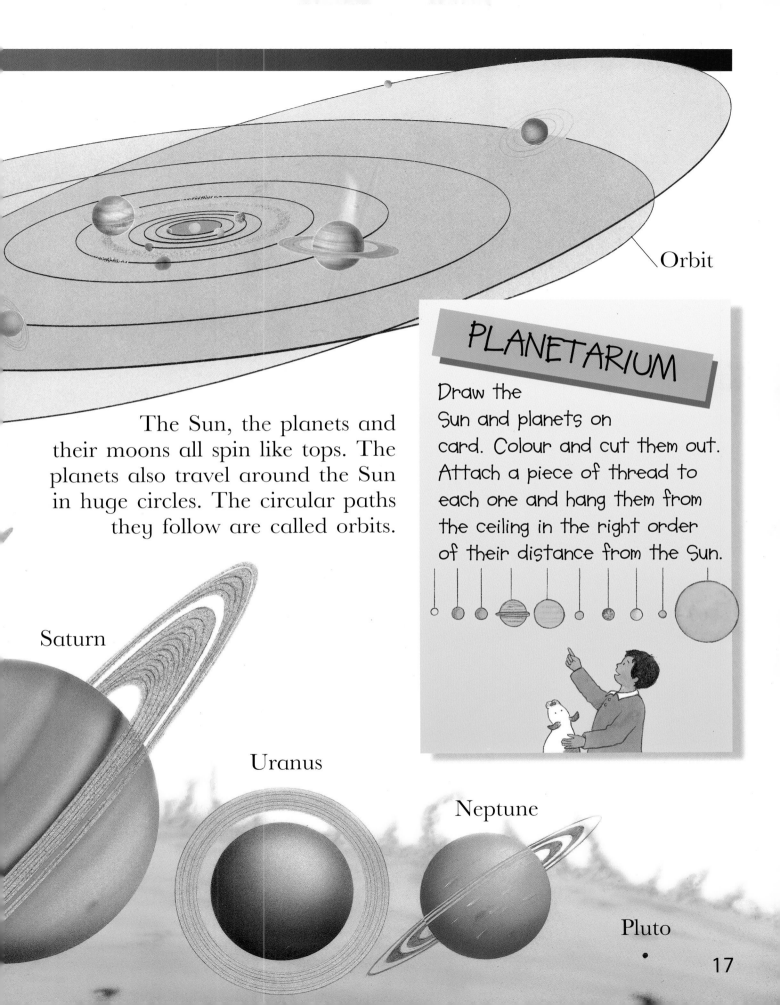

Orbit

The Sun, the planets and their moons all spin like tops. The planets also travel around the Sun in huge circles. The circular paths they follow are called orbits.

PLANETARIUM

Draw the Sun and planets on card. Colour and cut them out. Attach a piece of thread to each one and hang them from the ceiling in the right order of their distance from the Sun.

Saturn

Uranus

Neptune

Pluto

The Sun

The Sun is a star, just like the other stars you see in the sky at night. It is an enormous ball of burning gases, millions of times bigger than the Earth. The Sun sends out heat and light. Without it, the Earth would be cold, dark and lifeless.

The Sun's rays can damage your skin if you spend too long outside on a sunny day. People use special cream to protect their skin.

Sun

Earth

The Earth is the third planet from the Sun. It travels around it at a distance of about 150 million kilometres. The Earth moves very fast, but it still takes a year (365 days) to complete its orbit.

The Sun is mostly made of a gas called hydrogen. The hottest part of the Sun is its core. Hot gases bubble up to the surface. They form a halo of gases called the corona. The dark patches on the surface of the Sun are sunspots. They are cooler than the rest of its surface.

Flaming jets of gas can flare up from the surface of the Sun.

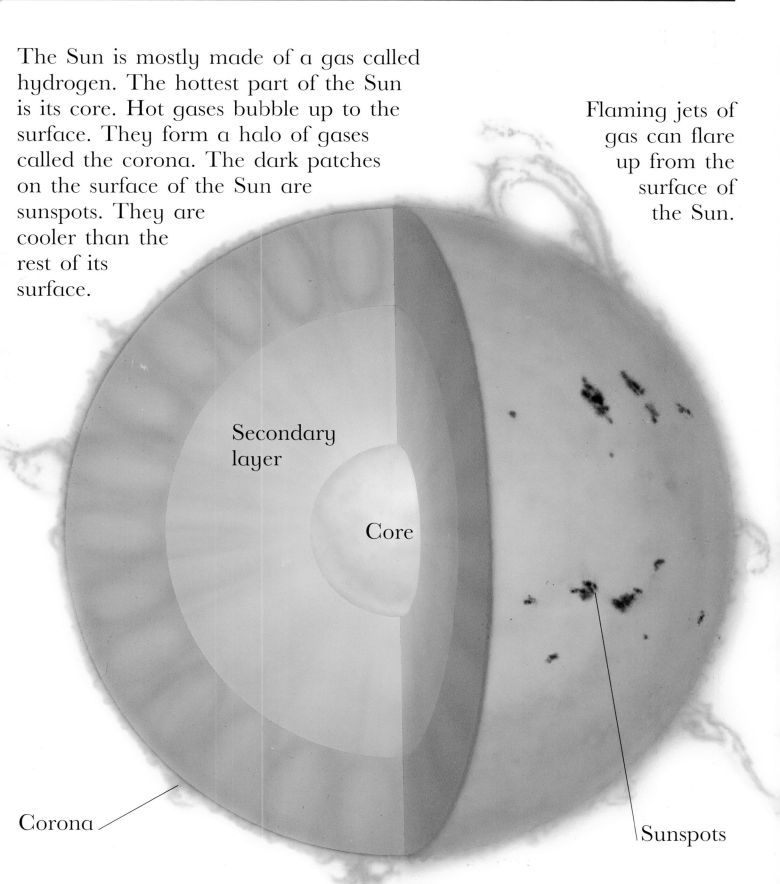

Secondary layer

Core

Corona

Sunspots

Close to the Sun

Mercury and Venus are the two planets in the Solar System that are closest to the Sun. They are both much, much hotter than the Earth. There are no signs of water on either planet. Nothing can grow or live on them.

Mercury spins very slowly, but it races around the Sun. It is burning hot on the side facing the Sun and icy cold on the opposite, dark side.

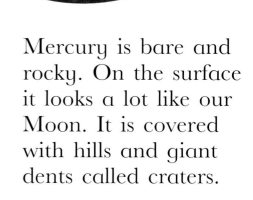

Mercury is bare and rocky. On the surface it looks a lot like our Moon. It is covered with hills and giant dents called craters.

Venus is about the same size as the Earth. It is the hottest planet of all. Its surface is covered by thick clouds of poisonous gases. These trap heat from the Sun.

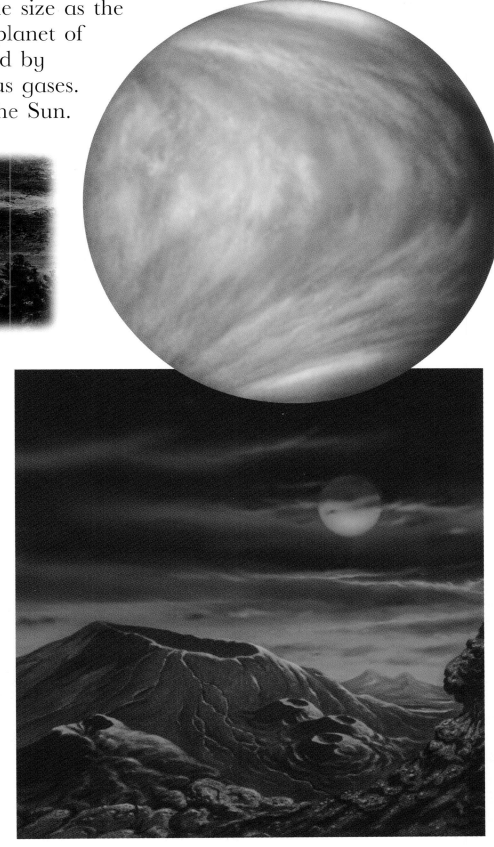

You can often see Venus shining brightly in the sky just after sunset or before sunrise. It always looks as if it is quite close to the Sun.

The surface of Venus is mainly flat, but there are lots of old volcanoes, and areas where lava has flowed from the volcanoes. Scientists think some of the volcanoes may still erupt from time to time.

The Earth

The Earth is the planet on which we live. It is a huge ball of rock spinning in space. The Earth is the only planet with water on it, and air for plants and animals to breathe. This is why there is life on Earth, but not on any other planet.

This is what the Earth looks like from out in space. Most of it is covered in blue sea. The brown and green areas are land. The white patterns are clouds swirling in the sky.

The Earth takes a day (24 hours) to spin round once. It is day on the side of the Earth facing the Sun. It is night on whichever side is facing away.

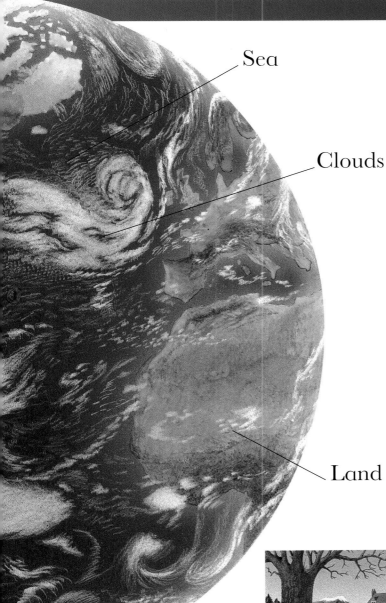

Sea

Clouds

Land

NIGHT AND DAY

Hold a globe and ask a friend to shine a torch at it. Then turn the globe. The torch is like the Sun. It is day in the area lit by the torch and night everywhere else.

Spring

Autumn

Summer

Winter

The Earth spins at an angle, so the seasons change as the Earth moves round the Sun. It is summer in the part of the world that is closest to the Sun.

The Moon

The Moon is the closest thing to us in space. It is a little over a quarter the size of the Earth, and takes about a month to travel around it. The Moon has no air, so nothing can grow on it or live there.

The Moon turns as it orbits the Earth, so that the same side of it is always facing the Earth. The dark areas on the Moon are plains.

The surface of the Moon is rocky and dusty. There are thousands of craters. These were made millions of years ago when large rocks from space crashed into the Moon.

New moon | Half moon, first quarter | Full moon | Half moon, last quarter | Crescent waning

The Moon seems to change shape. This is because we only see the part of it that is lit by the Sun. The sunlit part changes as the Moon moves around the Earth. Every month the Moon waxes (seems to grow bigger), then wanes (grows smaller).

MOON DIARY

Make a chart with a square for each day of the month. Draw and describe what the Moon looks like every night for a month.

Mars

Mars is the fourth planet from the Sun. It is the planet most like the Earth, but it is much colder because it is further from the Sun. A day on Mars is about the same length as a day on Earth. Mars also has summer and winter seasons.

Mars is often called 'the red planet' because its rocks are a rusty red colour. Winds and storms blow reddish dust about, making Mars look pink from Earth.

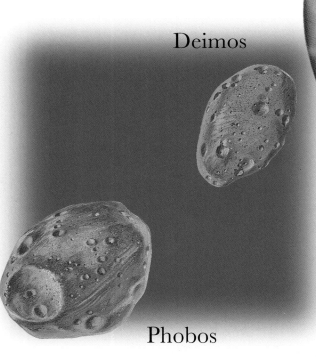

Deimos

Phobos

Mars is circled by two tiny, dark moons, called Phobos and Deimos. They are strangely shaped, rather like lumpy potatoes.

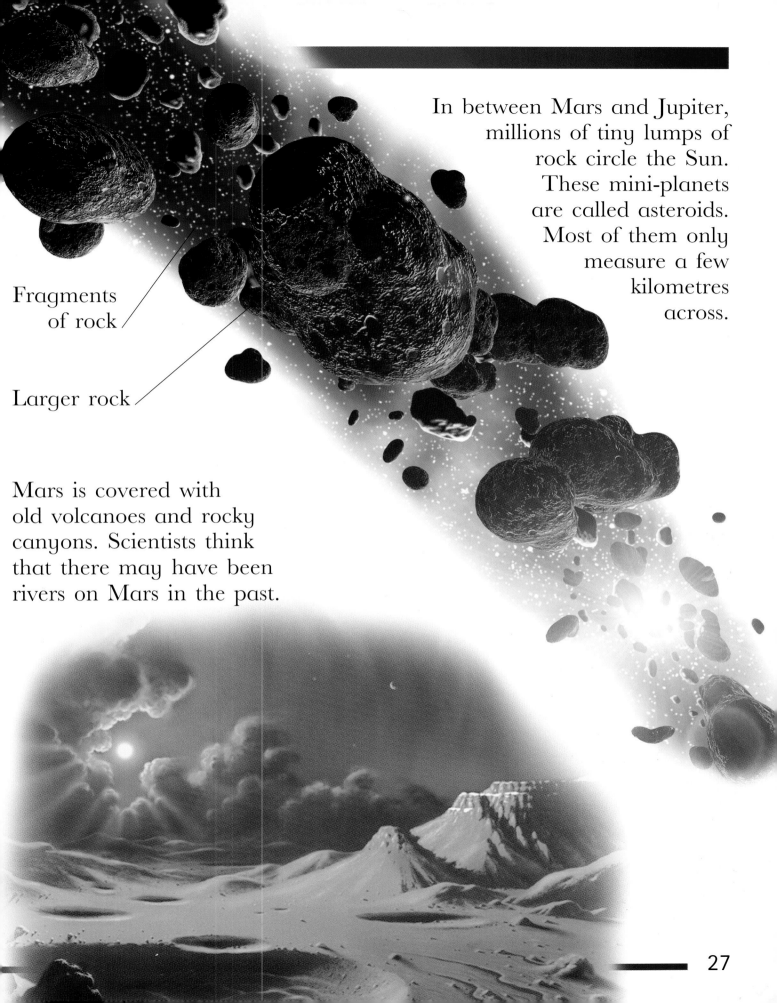

In between Mars and Jupiter, millions of tiny lumps of rock circle the Sun. These mini-planets are called asteroids. Most of them only measure a few kilometres across.

Fragments of rock

Larger rock

Mars is covered with old volcanoes and rocky canyons. Scientists think that there may have been rivers on Mars in the past.

The giant planets

Beyond the asteroids are two enormous gas planets, Jupiter and Saturn. Both of them are circled by rings and moons. Jupiter is the largest planet in the Solar System, larger than all the others put together.

Icy cold clouds cover the surface of Jupiter. Strong winds blow these into bands of different colours.

Swirling clouds

Jupiter has 16 moons. One of them, called Io, has active volcanoes on it. Io's rocky surface (left) is dyed red and orange by sulphur from its volcanoes.

Saturn is a spinning ball of gas and liquid. It is circled by 18 rocky moons. The planet's surface is covered in fast-moving clouds.

Icy rings

Strong winds race around Saturn.

Saturn's rings are really thousands of narrow ringlets. They are made of millions of bits of glittering ice. Most of these are tiny, but some measure several kilometres across.

MAKE JUPITER

Mix turpentine with drops of red and yellow oil paint. Put drops of colour in a tray of water and swirl them about with a paintbrush. Lay a circle of paper on top. Lift it off and hang it up to dry.

Distant planets

Out near the edge of the Solar System there are three planets; Uranus, Neptune and Pluto. They are so far away that they can't be seen with the naked eye. No space probe has visited Pluto, the most distant planet, so we do not know much about it.

Neptune is a blueish colour. It has eight moons. Its largest moon, Triton, is the coldest object in the Solar System. Its cracked, frozen surface is dotted with volcanoes. These erupt with plumes of black dust and gases.

Pluto is the smallest planet of all. It has one moon, called Charon, which is half its size. Pluto follows an oval-shaped orbit around the Sun. This means that it is sometimes closer to the Sun than Neptune.

Uranus is four times bigger than the Earth. It is circled by 15 moons and about 11 narrow rings of small rocks.

Moving stars

You can see many things in the sky that are not stars or planets. Meteors and comets are burning lumps of rock that look like streaks of light whizzing across the sky.

Meteors are often called shooting stars. Really, they are flecks of space dust which burn up in the air surrounding the Earth.

Lumps of space rock that crash into Earth are called meteorites. Some huge ones like this (right) make massive craters (left).

A comet hangs in the sky like a huge star with a tail. Comets are lumps of ice and rock that orbit the Sun. Their tails can be many millions of kilometres long.

Crumbling pieces of rock and ice

Nucleus

Jets of dust and gas

The Sun's heat melts the surface of the comet, making a cloud of gas and dust that blows into a giant tail.

Space discovery

One of the ways we find out more about the Universe is by sending spacecraft to explore. Fast rockets take satellites, probes and astronauts to study the planets and moons. These then send back new information to scientists on Earth.

Rockets are the only machines powerful enough to escape the Earth's 'pull' and travel into space. A rocket is made of parts called stages. Each stage has its own engine and fuel, and drops off once its fuel has run out.

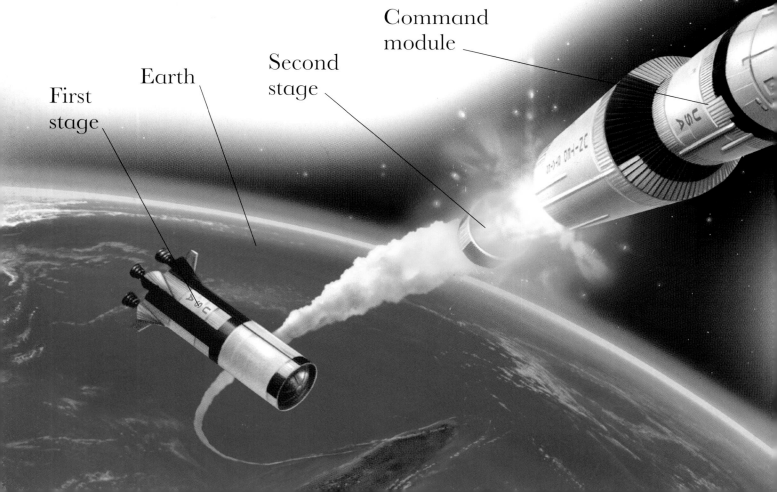

First stage

Earth

Second stage

Command module

Space probes are unmanned spacecraft that explore the Solar System. Mariner 10 (above) flew past Mercury three times and took thousands of photographs of its surface.

Spacecraft

LAUNCH PAD

Copy this rocket onto card and cut it out. Cut a strip of card and fold it as shown. Glue it to the rocket to make a stand.

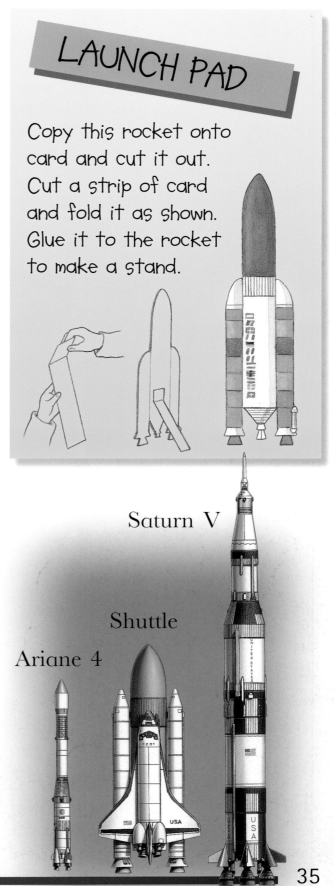

Saturn V

Shuttle

Ariane 4

Different-sized rockets are used to launch things into space. Ariane launches satellites and probes. The shuttle is launched by two rockets. Saturn V carried astronauts to the Moon.

Astronauts

Human beings cannot normally live in space. There is no air to breathe and everything is weightless. If astronauts are going to spend time in space, they must have air to breathe and the right living conditions.

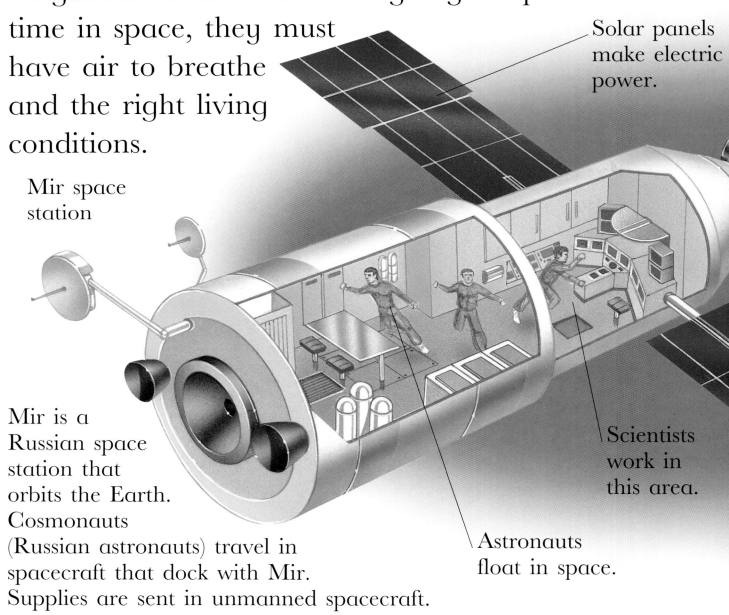

Mir space station

Solar panels make electric power.

Scientists work in this area.

Astronauts float in space.

Mir is a Russian space station that orbits the Earth. Cosmonauts (Russian astronauts) travel in spacecraft that dock with Mir. Supplies are sent in unmanned spacecraft.

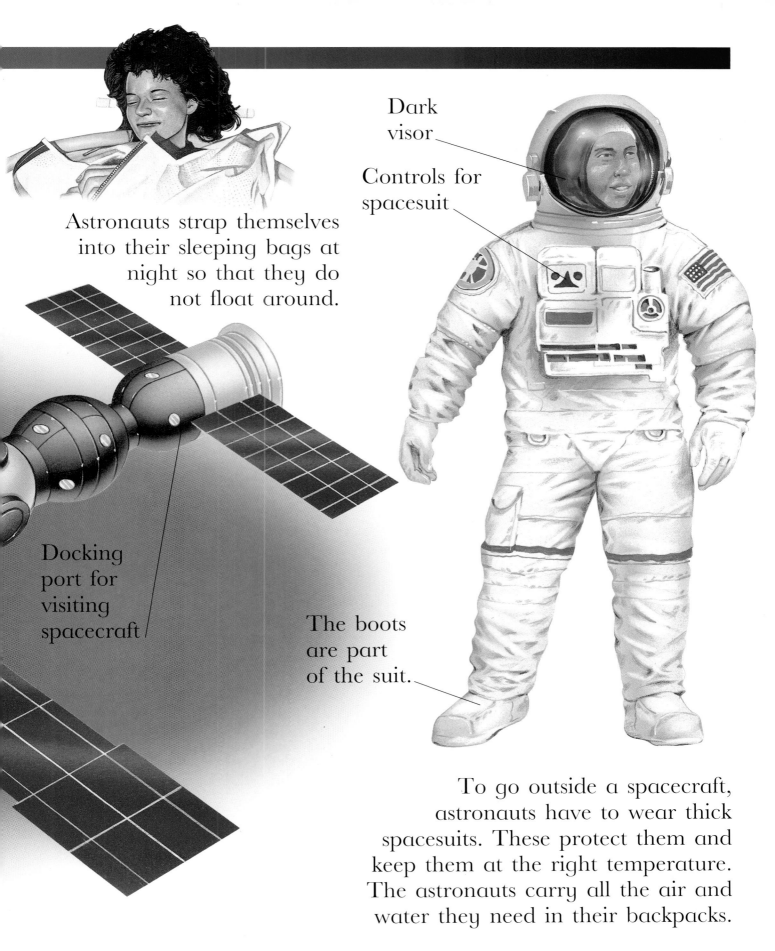

Astronauts strap themselves into their sleeping bags at night so that they do not float around.

Dark visor

Controls for spacesuit

Docking port for visiting spacecraft

The boots are part of the suit.

To go outside a spacecraft, astronauts have to wear thick spacesuits. These protect them and keep them at the right temperature. The astronauts carry all the air and water they need in their backpacks.

Space shuttle

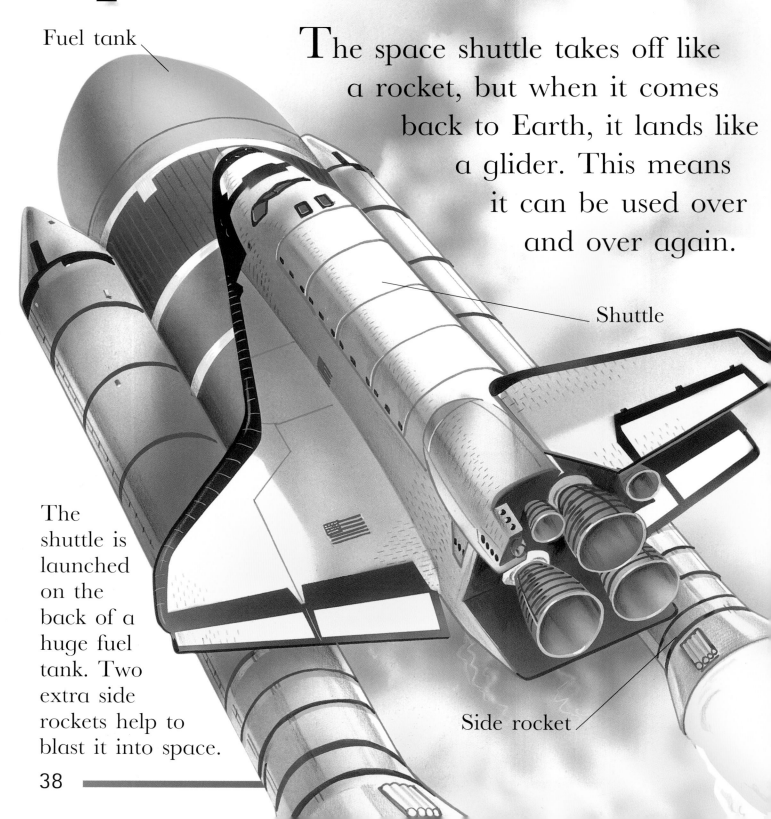

Fuel tank

The space shuttle takes off like a rocket, but when it comes back to Earth, it lands like a glider. This means it can be used over and over again.

Shuttle

The shuttle is launched on the back of a huge fuel tank. Two extra side rockets help to blast it into space.

Side rocket

The shuttle is covered with special tiles that stop it burning up as it speeds back to Earth.

Side rocket

After blast-off, the two side rockets drop back to Earth on huge parachutes.

ROCKET!

Thread a long piece of cotton through a straw. Tie the cotton to two chairs. Blow up a balloon and seal it with a bulldog clip. Tape the balloon to the straw. Open the clip and watch your rocket shoot forwards.

The World Around Us

About our world

The Earth is amazingly varied. It has hot deserts, huge oceans, steamy rainforests and frozen lands. Each part of the Earth has its own climate, or type of weather. Plants and animals adapt to where they live.

The landscape changes wherever you go. There are natural features, such as mountains. Landmarks such as oil wells have been made by people.

4

6

5

1

3

2

Most of our planet is covered by sea. There is a thin blanket of air surrounding the Earth. This gives us weather.

1. Sea
2. River
3. Lake
4. Rain
5. Waterfall
6. Mountain
7. Forest
8. Oil well
9. Animals
10. City

Volcano

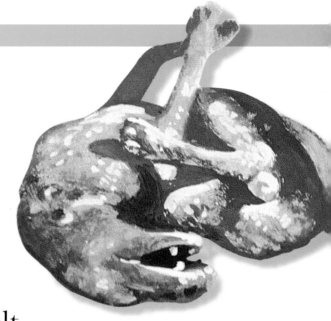

A volcano is a mountain that explodes. Deep beneath the surface of the Earth, the rocks are so hot that they melt. When a volcano erupts, this red-hot melted rock bursts out of a hole at the top of the mountain.

This dog was buried in the lava from a volcano in Pompeii, Italy, in AD79.

ERUPTION!

Make a cone of thick card, leaving a hole at the top. Put a shallow plastic pot in the hole. Add a little red powder paint and some bicarbonate of soda. Carefully add vinegar and watch the volcano erupt.

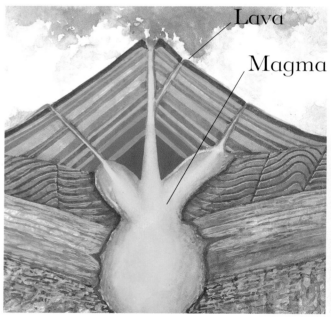

Lava

Magma

Hot, melted rock is called magma when it is under the ground, and lava when it reaches the surface.

During an eruption, boiling lava pours down the mountain sides, destroying anything in its path. The lava slowly cools in the air. Later it hardens into new rock.

Earthquakes

The top layer of the Earth, its crust, is like a giant jigsaw. It is made of huge interlocking pieces that move about very slowly all the time. Sometimes they do not move smoothly and this makes the ground shake. This is called an earthquake.

An earthquake is very frightening. The ground trembles and buildings may collapse, killing people. Earthquakes usually only last for a few minutes but they cause a lot of damage.

An earthquake happens when two of the Earth's plates, or pieces of its crust, try to move past each other and scrape together. They push and grind in opposite directions, making the rocks tilt and slip.

The shock waves from an earthquake often create giant waves called 'tsunamis', which speed across the sea. They tower up when they reach land, destroying whole villages and towns.

Earthquakes may cause fires because underground fuel lines are broken.

Huge cracks open up in the ground and swallow up cars.

Mountains

Mountains are the highest places on Earth. Some are so high that their peaks are hidden by the clouds. Many mountains are rocky and jagged, with deep valleys. Others are smaller and more rounded.

The higher up a mountain you go, the colder and more windy it is. Trees cannot grow above a certain height, known as the tree line. Further up high mountains, there is snow on the ground all year.

Mountain goats have specially adapted hooves so that they can scramble up and down the steepest mountain sides without slipping.

Mountain plants, such as this gentian, grow close to the ground so that they cannot be damaged by the wind.

Like all mountain animals, the Alpine hare has a thick coat of fur to keep it warm.

Shaping the land

The landscape is slowly changing all the time. It is worn away by water and the wind. The sea makes cliffs, and rivers carve out valleys. Even the hardest rocks are worn down.

In a desert, sand is blown around by the wind. It rubs against rocks, wearing them into amazing shapes.

Water trickling through limestone creates underground caves with huge stalactites and stalagmites.

50

The Grand Canyon is a giant gorge in the United States. It has been carved out of the rocks over thousands of years by the Colorado River. As the river has worked its way downwards, it has exposed different layers of rock. The lower down the canyon the layer of rock is, the older it is.

Weather

The weather changes from day to day, and from season to season. It may be sunny one day and rainy the next. If the Sun comes out when it is raining, you may see a rainbow. The weather is also different in other parts of the world. Some places are always hot and others are freezing cold.

Flashes of lightning are giant sparks of electricity that jump between storm clouds and the ground. Thunder is the loud noise that the lightning makes.

The colours in a rainbow are always in the same order – red, orange, yellow, green, blue, indigo and violet.

Clouds are made of millions of tiny drops of water. Some are a sign of fine weather. Others bring rain or thunderstorms.

Cirrus

Stratus

Cumulonimbus

Cumulus

WEATHER CHART

Draw a grid on a large piece of paper and mark out the days of the week. Look at the weather every day and fill in the correct weather symbol on your chart.

Sunny Cloudy Rainy Windy

Some countries have violent storms called tornadoes. A tornado looks like a dark funnel of cloud. In fact, it is a whirlwind that spins along the ground and causes terrible damage. Fast winds whirl around a central funnel where there is hardly any wind at all.

Water cycle

The air is full of tiny drops of water too small to see, called water vapour. Rain does not just come from the sky, but from the water that is all around us. The amount of water on Earth stays the same, but it keeps moving around.

The clouds grow heavier and are blown over the land.

Water vapour rises and forms clouds.

Water from the sea turns to water vapour.

As water is warmed by the Sun, it seems to dry up. In fact, it has risen into the air as water vapour. As water vapour rises, it cools down and turns back into drops of water. These form clouds and it rains.

If it is cold, there may be snow instead of rain. The drops of water in the clouds freeze into ice crystals and these join together to make delicate snowflakes. No two snowflakes are ever the same.

Water in the clouds falls as rain, hail, sleet or snow.

Rainwater runs into rivers and flows back into the sea.

MAKE A SNOW STORM

Find a jar with a tight screw-top. Glue cake decorations inside the lid. Pour water into the jar until it is nearly full. Add some glitter and screw on the lid. Shake the jar and turn it upside down.

Life of a river

Many rivers start life in the mountains. Streams of rainwater run from high to low land. They join together and grow into a river. This flows downhill towards the sea.

A river provides food for all kinds of creatures. There are many fish, such as this salmon.

Rain falls high in the mountains.

Streams run into each other.

Waterfall

A river changes with each stage of its journey. It starts life as a bubbling stream, but by the time it reaches the sea it is wider and flows much more slowly.

The river grows wider.

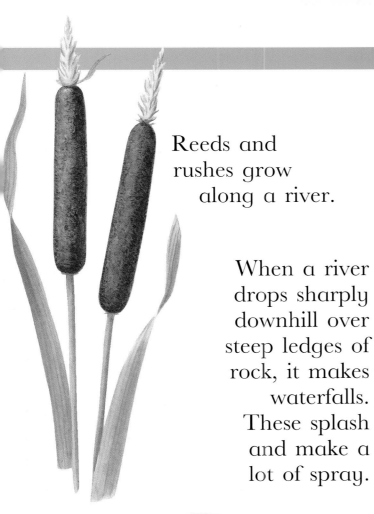

Reeds and rushes grow along a river.

When a river drops sharply downhill over steep ledges of rock, it makes waterfalls. These splash and make a lot of spray.

The river winds its way across the land.

All rivers end at the sea. The place where a river flows out into the sea is called the river's mouth.

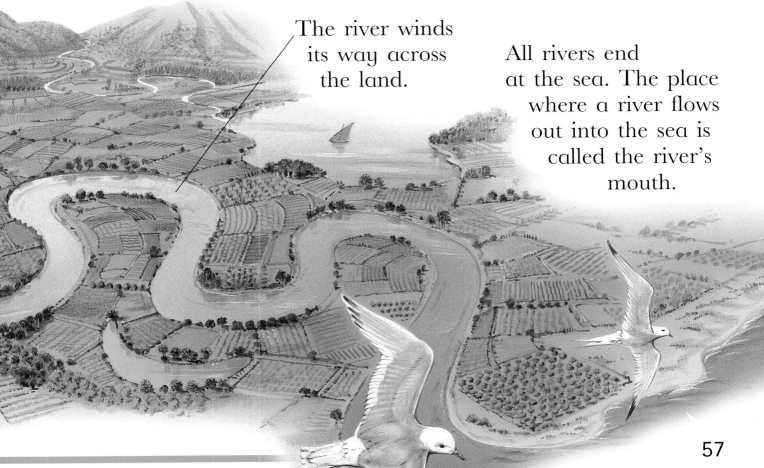

Marshes

Marshes and swamps are wet, boggy areas of land next to rivers or the sea. Some of them look like lakes dotted with islands. Others look more like grasslands because so many reeds grow there.

1. Mangrove roots
2. Raccoon
3. Terrapin
4. Roseate spoonbill
5. Alligator
6. Tarpon
7. Zebra butterfly
8. Woodpecker
9. Rough green snake
10. Green tree frog

Marshes are home to many exotic birds and animals. The tree roots and reeds make good homes, and there are lots of fish to eat in the water.

DRAGONFLY

Template

Copy the dragonfly template onto a large piece of paper. Glue foil sweet papers onto the body and wings. Use buttons for the eyes and pipe cleaners for the antennae.

Woodlands

Woods grow in parts of the world where it is never very hot or very cold. In the summer it is green and shady, but when the trees lose their leaves in winter the wood looks bare. Woods provide food and homes for many different animals.

Birds and squirrels shelter high in the trees. Badgers and foxes dig burrows beneath the tree roots. Deer and boar hide amongst the bushes and shrubs.

1. Fox
2. Jay
3. Wild boar
4. Porcupine
5. Sparrow hawk
6. Grey squirrel
7. Red deer
8. Speckled wood butterfly
9. Badger
10. Great spotted woodpecker

Rainforest

Steamy rainforests grow in hot countries where it rains nearly every day. It is hot all the year round, so there is no summer or winter. More plants and animals live in rainforests than anywhere else in the world.

Colourful parrots roost in the treetops.

The trees in a rainforest grow huge because it rains so much. It is dark and shady down on the ground, but bright and sunny in the treetops. There, high above the ground, the branches lace together to form a canopy where flowers and fruit grow.

Bushbabies and other small animals come out at night to hunt for food.

The largest hunters in a rainforest are big cats, such as this tiger.

Look for all these
things in the
big picture.

1. Creeper
2. Gibbon
3. Poison dart frog
4. Toadstools
5. Macaw
6. Butterflies
7. Leaf-cutter ants
8. Toucan

Grasslands

Around the world there are huge grasslands that stretch for thousands of kilometres. After it rains the grass is green, but for most of the year it is dry and brown. It does not rain often enough for many trees to grow here.

The savannas in Africa are enormous grassy plains dotted with a few thorny bushes and trees. Many wild animals live there. They move around to find water and the freshest green grass.

The North American grasslands are called prairies. Prairie dogs are mammals that live on prairies and burrow under the ground to make their homes. One prairie dog always guards the burrow entrance.

1. Gazelles
2. Giraffes
3. Zebra
4. Elephant
5. Lioness and cub
6. Eland (antelope)

Deserts

Deserts are the driest places on Earth. Sometimes there is no rain for years. Most deserts are burning hot during the day and freezing cold at night. Some are cold all the time. They are often home to some unusual plants and animals.

1. Elf owl
2. Gila woodpecker
3. Saguaro cactus
4. Bearded lizard

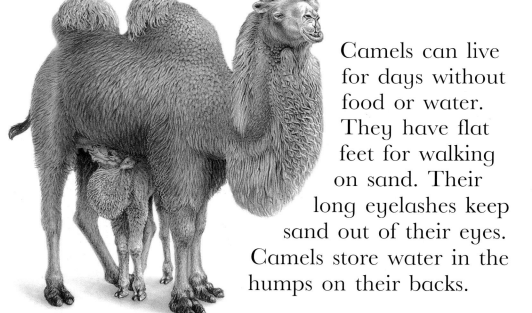

Camels can live for days without food or water. They have flat feet for walking on sand. Their long eyelashes keep sand out of their eyes. Camels store water in the humps on their backs.

The American deserts are bare and rocky. Spiky plants called cacti grow there. They store water in their fat stems.

1

Some deserts are sandy. Strong winds blow the sand into hills called dunes. The only places where plants and trees grow is near waterholes, called oases.

5. Rattlesnake
6. Roadrunner
7. Kangaroo rat
8. Kit fox

SAND PICTURE

Draw a picture of a desert on stiff, coloured paper with a glue stick. Pour sand over the glue. Tip off the loose sand to see the picture you have made.

Cold lands

The North and South Poles are at the top and bottom of the Earth. The land and sea around them are frozen. They are covered in snow and ice all the year round.

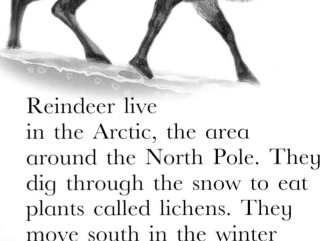

Reindeer live in the Arctic, the area around the North Pole. They dig through the snow to eat plants called lichens. They move south in the winter to find more food.

Penguins bring up their chicks on frozen seas near the South Pole.

The Arctic hare's fur turns white in winter.

The polar
bear is the
biggest hunter in the
Arctic. Its thick, oily coat
keeps it warm. Polar bears are
good swimmers. They hunt for seals
beneath the ice, or wait for them by
blowholes where the seals come up for air.

Saving our planet

There are many problems facing our planet. The air and seas are becoming dirty, or polluted. Plants and animals are dying out. The Earth's natural fuels, such as gas, coal and oil, are being used up.

Fumes from factories and cars pollute the air with chemicals. These dissolve in clouds and make acid rain, which falls to the ground and harms wildlife and plants.

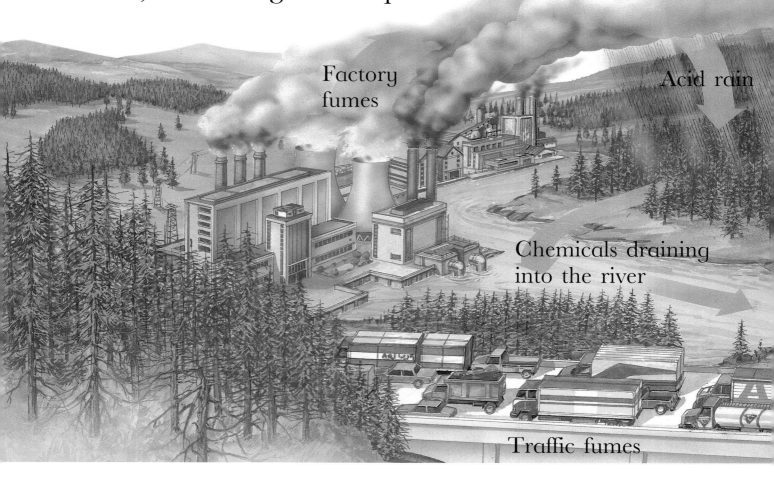

Factory fumes

Acid rain

Chemicals draining into the river

Traffic fumes

Scientists are inventing new forms of energy that do not cause pollution. They can use energy from the Sun or wind to make electricity.

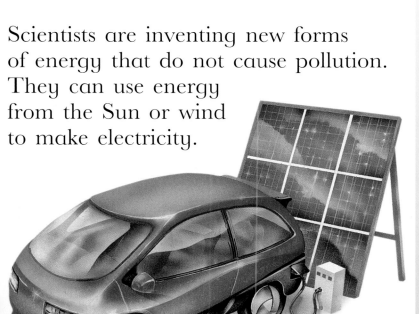

Solar-powered electric car

RECYCLE IT!

Sort your family's rubbish into boxes for paper, glass and aluminium cans. Take them to your local recycling centre.

Animals are hunted and their homes are destroyed or polluted. The humpback whale (below) has been hunted so much that it may die out.

Humpback whale

Prehistoric Life

Clues to the past

Scientists find out about the history of the Earth by studying rocks. The remains of plants and animals that lived long ago have turned to stone and become fossils. They give us clues about what lived on Earth millions of years ago.

Plant-eating Triceratops

No one has ever seen a dinosaur. Scientists work out what they looked like by putting together the fossils they find. Fossils take thousands of years to form. They are usually the hard bits of the body, such as bones and teeth.

Flat tooth of a plant-eating dinosaur

Meat-eating Tyrannosaurus Rex

Sharp teeth of a meat-eater

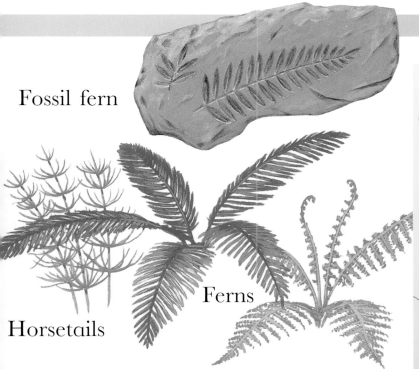

Fossil fern

Horsetails

Ferns

The fossil print on the rock above was made by a fern hundreds of millions of years ago. It looks like the ferns that grow today. Scientists have also found fossils of horsetails, another plant that still exists.

MAKE A FOSSIL

Shape some modelling clay into a square. Press a leaf into it to make a fossil print. Peel the leaf off, then bury the modelling clay 'fossil' in a tray of dry sand. Brush off the sand to reveal the fossil.

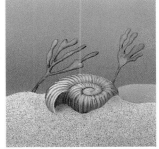

Millions of years ago, shellfish called ammonites lived in the sea. When they died, they were buried in mud and sand. As more layers of mud built up, the ammonites slowly turned to rock, becoming fossils.

Ammonite fossil

Evolution

The Earth is millions of years old and is slowly changing all the time. As the Earth changes, so do the plants and animals that live here. They adapt to suit where they live. The way that living things change is called evolution.

The first tiny fish lived in the sea about 500 million years ago.

About 395 million years ago some animals moved on to the land. These were the amphibians.

Nearly all of the animals that live on Earth today did not exist in the past. Most of the animals that lived in the past no longer exist today. The first plants and animals were tiny and lived in the sea. Nowadays there are all sorts of living things on every part of the planet.

Some animals die out, or become extinct, if their homes and lives are disturbed. The dodo was a large flightless bird that lived on the island of Mauritius. It was hunted by the people who first settled on the island and is now extinct.

Dinosaurs and other reptiles lived from 240 million years ago to 64 million years ago.

After the dinosaurs died out, there were more mammals. The first ones were small, but later ones were bigger.

The first humans lived about two million years ago. They may have evolved from ape-like creatures.

First life

The first plants and animals lived in the sea. They were probably too small to see. The first animals had soft bodies, like jellyfish and worms. Soon there were animals with hard shells. The first fish appeared after this.

Many different sea creatures lived around a coral reef about 450 million years ago. They swam or crept along the seabed in search of things to eat.

1. Trilobite
2. Brachiopods
3. Graptolite

Fish were the first animals with bones. Duncleosteus was a monster fish. It was a fierce hunter with huge sharp teeth.

4. Sea scorpion
5. Horn coral
6. Sea snail
7. Sea lily
8. Nautiloid

AMMONITE ART

Draw an ammonite on a piece of white paper with a white wax crayon, copying the picture below. Paint all over the picture with blue-green paint. Your picture of the ammonite will appear where the wax crayon lines are.

On to the land

About 400 million years ago, plants started to grow on land. Then some fish began to crawl out of the water and on to land. They dragged themselves along on their strong, stubby fins. Before long, amphibians lived on the land, but had to return to the water to lay their eggs.

In a freshwater swamp 360 million years ago, small fish scuttle ashore. On the banks is an amphibian called Ichthyostega. This was one of the first-known animals with four legs, but it still had webbed feet and a fishy tail.

1. Ichthyostega
2. Meganeura
3. Rhipidistians
4. Eusthenopteron
5. Horsetails

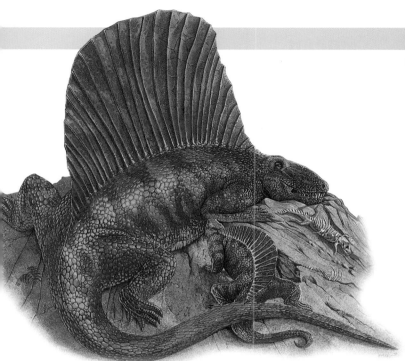

Dimetrodon was one of the first reptiles and it lived on land. It had a huge sail of skin on its back.

MAKE A PALM TREE

Roll up a newspaper and tie two elastic bands around it, as shown. Make four cuts in the top third of the roll and pull back the cut ends.

5

4

Dinosaur world

Dinosaurs appeared on our planet 228 million years ago. Some of them were enormous. They were the biggest animals ever to live on land. Others were not much bigger than a chicken. All of them died out 64 million years ago.

All dinosaurs had scaly skins and laid eggs, like reptiles do today. Some ate plants, while others were hunters. They lived alongside other reptiles and early kinds of birds and insects.

Many dinosaurs
lived near swamps.

1. Stegosaurus
2. Apatosaurus
3. Deinosuchus
4. Allosaurus
5. Archaeopteryx

Plant-eaters

The biggest dinosaurs of all were plant-eaters. They had barrel-shaped bodies and very long necks and tails. These giants lived in herds and moved from place to place looking for food. They plucked leaves from high in trees, like giraffes do today.

The weather was warm and wet at the time of the dinosaurs. There were forests of giant ferns and evergreens. Plant-eaters ate leaves, roots and pine cones. They had peg-like teeth for snipping leaves off trees.

1. Brachiosaurus
2. Apatosaurus
3. Diplodocus

Some plant-eaters looked very strange. One was called Parasaurolophus. These dinosaurs had mouths like beaks and bony crests on their heads. They could blow out through these, and may have tooted like trombones.

2

3

DINOSAUR INVITE

Draw and colour a long-necked dinosaur on a wide piece of card. Write your party instructions on the back. Make it into a concertina shape by folding the card as shown.

Meat-eaters

Some dinosaurs ate animals and other dinosaurs. Most meat-eaters were very fierce and could move fast to catch their prey. Some of them hunted alone. Others hunted in packs.

Tyrannosaurus Rex was the biggest meat-eater of all. It had massive jaws and razor-sharp teeth for slicing through flesh.

Many meat-eaters had huge hooked claws for slashing out at the animals they chased.

Meat-eating dinosaurs did not need to eat every day. One kill would provide enough food for several days. Some dinosaurs did not hunt at all. Instead they were scavengers, eating any dead or dying animals that they found.

Afrovenator ate plant-eating dinosaurs and other, smaller animals

Into battle

Plant-eating dinosaurs could not move fast, so they had to be able to defend themselves against hungry meat-eaters. Some plant-eaters grouped together for safety. Others had fierce horns to scare off enemies, and thick skin like armour.

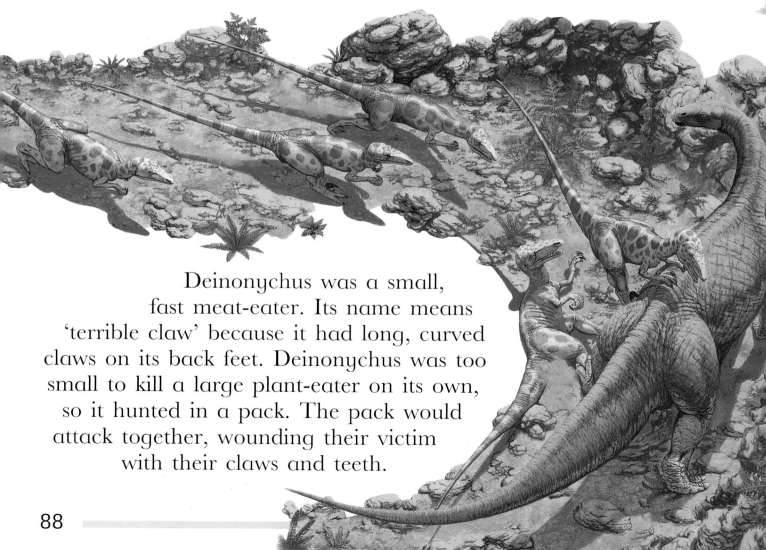

Deinonychus was a small, fast meat-eater. Its name means 'terrible claw' because it had long, curved claws on its back feet. Deinonychus was too small to kill a large plant-eater on its own, so it hunted in a pack. The pack would attack together, wounding their victim with their claws and teeth.

Triceratops was armed with horns on its nose and above its eyes. It also had a huge bony neck shield and thick, leathery skin to protect it from enemies.

This armoured dinosaur was called Euoplocephalus. It had bony plates and spikes along its back and a huge club at the end of its tail.

A TRICERATOPS MASK

Draw a Triceratops face like this on thick card. Make a nose horn out of card and attach it to the mask with a paper fastener.

Tie a thin piece of elastic through holes at the sides of the mask.

Hatching out

Dinosaur babies hatched from eggs, just as reptiles do today. Some dinosaur mothers, including Maiasaura, made big nests on the ground in which they laid about 20 eggs. In 1984, a group of more than 20 Maiasaura nests was found on Egg Mountain in the United States.

Dinosaur eggs

Fossils of dinosaur eggs are found in different shapes and sizes.

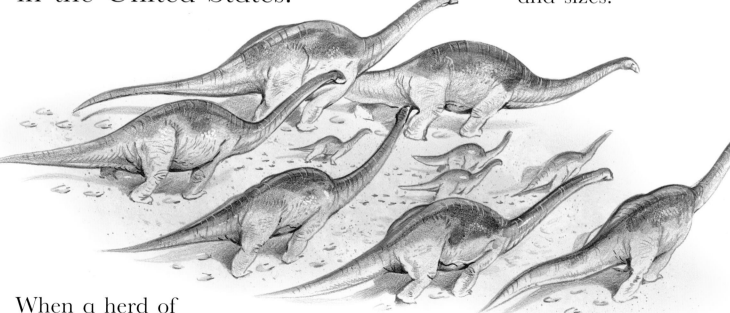

When a herd of long-necked dinosaurs set off, the little ones walked in the middle, guarded by the enormous grown-ups.

When Maiasaura babies
hatched out, their mother
brought them tender
young plants to eat.
After a few weeks,
the babies could look
for their own food.

This baby dinosaur is
curled up inside its egg.

Nest built
inside
an earth
mound

Giants of the sea

While dinosaurs ruled the land, many fierce reptiles lived in the sea. Some of them were fast swimmers and looked like dolphins. Others were like lizards, or had strange long necks and giant flippers like paddles.

Kronosaurus had a huge head bigger than a car.

Mosasaurus was a fierce sea lizard. It crunched small sea creatures in its powerful jaws.

Elasmosaurus had
a long snake-like neck.
It may have swum along
holding its neck and tiny
head above the water.

Ichthyosaurus looked
like one of today's
dolphins. It was a
fast swimmer and
might have hunted in
shoals. It ate fish and
creatures like squid.

Teleosaurus was a sea crocodile.
It was quick to snap up fish in its long
snout, which was armed with sharp teeth.

Take to the skies

The first creatures to fly were insects, 300 million years ago. Then reptiles called pterosaurs took to the air. They glided through the skies, soaring above the dinosaurs on the land.

Archaeopteryx was the first creature with feathers. It was half-dinosaur and half-bird. No one knows if it could fly.

Quetzalcoatlus was a giant pterosaur, much, much bigger than even the largest birds today. Its huge wings were made of skin, like a bat's wings. It had a furry body and no feathers or teeth.

The first insects with wings were dragonflies. Meganeura was a huge dragonfly with a wingspan of about 75 centimetres.

FLY A PTEROSAUR

Tie two canes together, one twice as long as the other. Ask an adult to cut notches in the ends. Tie a piece of string to each corner to make a frame. Lay the frame on a clear plastic bag. Cut around it, 5 cm outside. Stretch the bag across the frame and tape the edges down. Cut out a pterosaur and tape it to the kite. Tie on some string.

Extinction

Dinosaurs lived on the Earth for 165 million years before they became extinct, dying out for ever. All the flying reptiles, sea reptiles and many other animals died out at the same time. No one knows exactly why.

There are many ideas about why the dinosaurs disappeared. Some people think that mammals might have stolen and eaten too many dinosaur eggs. Others think that the weather and living conditions changed, and that it may have become too hot or too cold for the dinosaurs.

Scientists think that a giant meteorite crashed into the Earth about 65 million years ago. Dust from the crash may have blocked out the Sun, so that it was cold and no plants could grow. Plant-eating animals would have starved to death. Meat-eaters would have soon died out too, when there were no other animals for them to eat.

Fur and feathers

After all the dinosaurs died out, mammals and birds became more common. Unlike dinosaurs, both are warm-blooded. Mammals have fur or hair, and give birth to live babies. Birds have feathers to keep them warm.

Saghatherium was about the size of a lion, but very shy. It ate grass and had tiny hooves on its toes.

Not all mammals lived on land. Desmostylus looked rather like a walrus and had long tusks. It spent most of its time hunting for fish in the sea, but came ashore to have its babies.

Hyracotherium was one
of the first horses. It was tiny,
not much bigger than a cat.
Instead of hooves, it had four
toes on each front foot and
three toes on its back feet.

Diatryma was a huge bird with
a beak like a parrot's. It could
not fly, but it could run fast.

Smilodon was
a big, fierce
sabre-toothed
cat. It killed
its victims
by stabbing
them with
its dagger-like
front teeth.

First people

For most of the Earth's history, there have been no humans. The first people like us lived only about 100,000 years ago. They may have been related to ape-like creatures that lived earlier.

People living 15,000 years ago survived by hunting, fishing and gathering plants to eat. They moved from place to place in search of food, and sheltered in caves or tents.

Making a fire

Some people lived in caves. They painted pictures of the animals they hunted on their cave walls, using colours made from crushed rocks.

People hunted woolly mammoths. They were huge and had long, thick hair to protect them from the cold weather.

A WOOLLY MAMMOTH

Draw a big woolly mammoth on a large piece of thick paper or card, copying the picture on the right. Colour in its tusks, toes and eyes. To make its hairy coat, cut short pieces of reddish-brown wool and glue them to your picture. If you want to, you can cut it out.

Making tools

Early people were good at making things with their hands. Remains found in their caves show that they made knives and weapons from sharp stones and tools from antlers, bones and mammoth tusks.

Plant Life

Plants everywhere

There are millions of different kinds of plants and they grow nearly everywhere in the world. They can be all shapes and sizes, from tiny mosses to enormous trees. Some spring up after rain in hot, dry deserts. Others flower in snowy cracks high on mountains.

In steamy rainforests, many plants grow high above the ground on sunny tree branches. These plants are called epiphytes. They soak up all the water they need from the damp air or collect rainwater in their cup-shaped leaves.

Like many plants, the rose has beautiful flowers. Roses often smell sweet.

Oak tree

Acorn

Trees are the largest plants in the world. Some, such as the oak, can live to be hundreds of years old. The oak produces seeds called acorns.

Fungi are very unusual plants. They do not have leaves or roots, and they are not green. Instead of seeds, they produce spores.

Some plants live underwater. Thick forests of rubbery seaweed grow in sand and mud at the bottom of the sea.

Food for growth

Plants need food and water to grow. Their roots take water from the soil and their leaves soak up air and sunlight. Plants use water, air and sunlight to make their own food.

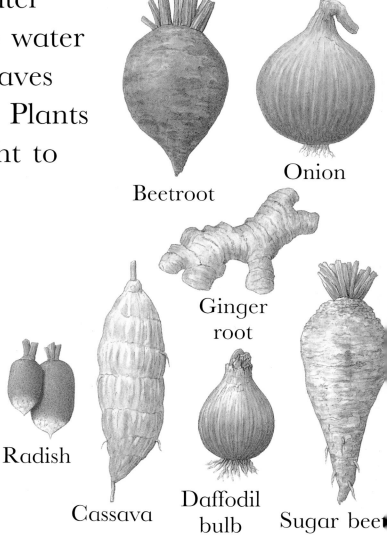

Beetroot

Onion

Ginger root

Radish

Cassava

Daffodil bulb

Sugar beet

TAKE A CUTTING

Spider plants grow baby plants at the ends of runners. Snip off a baby plant and put it in a glass of water. When it has grown roots, plant it in a small pot of moist compost.

All plants have roots. Some plants have fat roots, others have swollen buds or stems under the ground. These are a kind of food store. Plants use the food stored in them to grow when conditions are right.

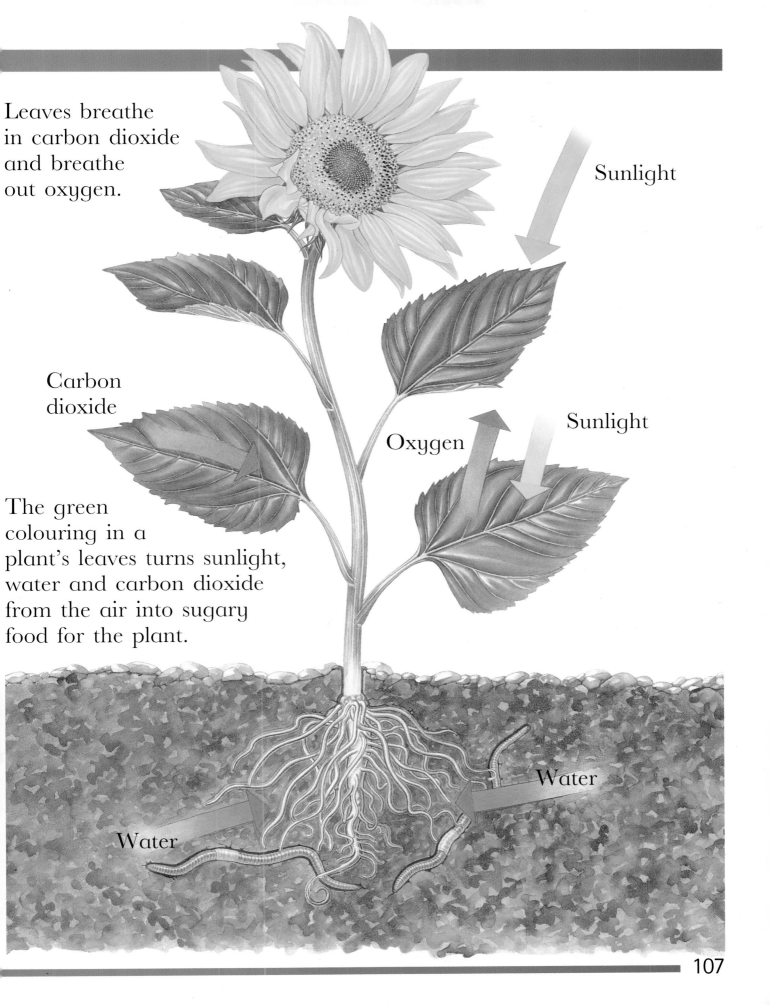

Leaves breathe in carbon dioxide and breathe out oxygen.

Sunlight

Carbon dioxide

Sunlight

Oxygen

The green colouring in a plant's leaves turns sunlight, water and carbon dioxide from the air into sugary food for the plant.

Water

Water

Flowers

There are flowers of nearly every colour, and many different shapes – bells, circles, stars and trumpets. Garden flowers are are often the showy relatives of simple wild flowers.

A meadow is full of flowers in the spring and summer. Butterflies and other insects visit the flowers because they like their colour and scent.

Buttercups

Poppies

Some flowers, like this orchid, are rare and only grow in a few places. It is important not to pick rare plants so that they can make seeds for new plants.

PRESS FLOWERS

Lay fresh flowers between pieces of blotting paper in a book. Shut the book and put something heavy on top. Leave for four weeks, then glue the flowers to cards and bookmarks.

Daisies

Clover

Making seeds

To make seeds, a flower needs pollen from another flower. Most flowers contain a sweet juice called nectar to attract birds and insects. As they drink, they brush against pollen, which they carry from flower to flower. This is called pollination.

Tiny hummingbirds pollinate some flowers in hot countries. They push their beaks right into the flowers to reach the nectar inside.

Pollen

Hibiscus flowers attract hummingbirds.

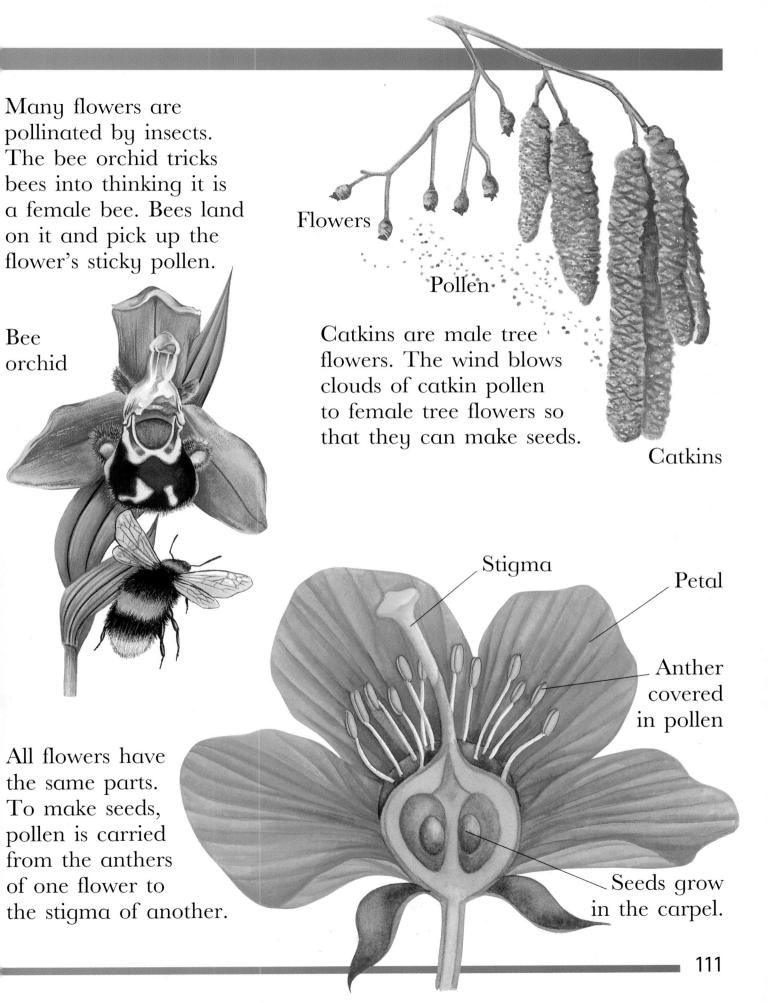

Many flowers are pollinated by insects. The bee orchid tricks bees into thinking it is a female bee. Bees land on it and pick up the flower's sticky pollen.

Bee orchid

Flowers

Pollen

Catkins are male tree flowers. The wind blows clouds of catkin pollen to female tree flowers so that they can make seeds.

Catkins

Stigma

Petal

Anther covered in pollen

All flowers have the same parts. To make seeds, pollen is carried from the anthers of one flower to the stigma of another.

Seeds grow in the carpel.

Fruits and berries

After a flower has been pollinated, seeds start to grow. They are protected by a soft fruit which grows around the seeds. Some fruits only contain one big seed or pip. Berries have lots of tiny seeds inside them.

In the autumn, hedges are full of ripe, juicy berries. These are eaten by birds and animals. Later, the seeds inside the berries are scattered on the ground in bird and animal droppings.

Look for these berries in the picture:

1. Hawthorn berries
2. Rosehips
3. Blackberries
4. Elderberries
5. Rowan berries

4

5

PUMPKIN HEAD!

Ask an adult to slice off the top of a pumpkin. Scoop out the flesh.

Cut holes in the pumpkin to make it look like a face. Cut a small hole in the lid.

Wedge a safety candle in the base of the pumpkin and ask an adult to light it for you.

All trees make fruits. These contain seeds that can grow into new trees. Some fruits, such as oranges, are soft. Nuts are tree fruits with hard shells around them.

Orange tree

Seeds

Most plants grow from seeds which fall on the ground. In spring, the soil is damp and warm. This makes each seed swell and start to grow. The root grows first, then a shoot. This is called germination.

Seeds inside berries often reach the ground in birds' droppings.

Dandelion seeds are blown to the ground by the wind.

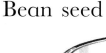

Bean seed

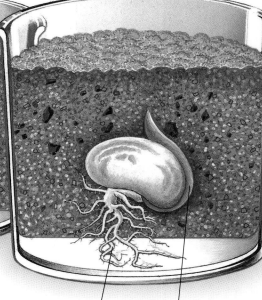

Root Shoot

When a seed germinates, it splits open and a root begins to grow. A leafy shoot pushes up through the soil towards the light. Leaves help the plant to make its own food.

First real leaves

Stem

Put some tissue paper in two clean eggshells. Sprinkle cress seeds on top and keep the tissue damp. In ten days you will be able to cut some cress.

Some seeds are hidden inside soft, juicy fruit. Others have hard shells to protect them and are called nuts.

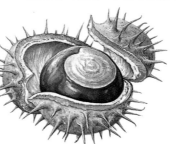

Horse chestnut

Peach

Pine cone

Sycamore

Trees

Trees are the biggest plants in the world. They have strong woody trunks and branches. There are two main kinds of tree. Deciduous trees lose their leaves in winter. Evergreens have leaves all year round.

Deciduous leaves often change colour in autumn.

Horse chestnut flowers

Horse chestnut fruit (conker)

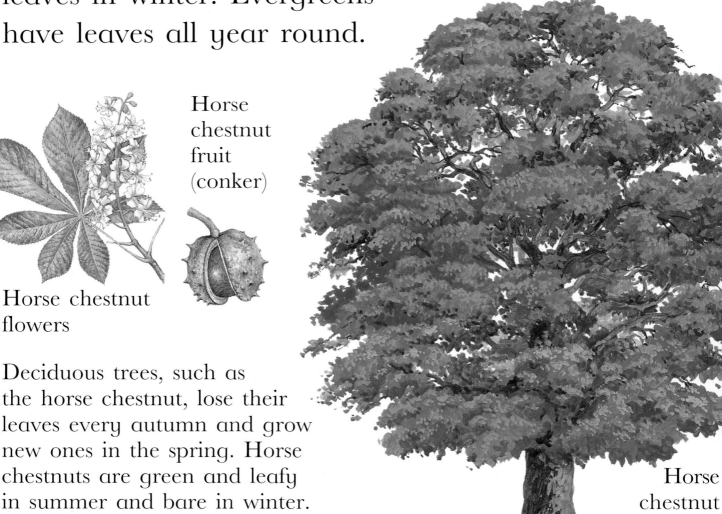

Horse chestnut

Deciduous trees, such as the horse chestnut, lose their leaves every autumn and grow new ones in the spring. Horse chestnuts are green and leafy in summer and bare in winter.

MAKE BARK RUBBINGS

Tape a piece of paper to a tree. Rub a wax crayon up and down the paper, using the flat side of the crayon.

Some evergreens are called conifers because they have cones.

Evergreens, such as the spruce, have long, thin leaves with a hard, waxy surface. These are called needles. They stay on the tree for several years before they drop off, though they never all fall off at the same time.

Spruce

Ferns and fungi

Ferns, fungi, mosses and lichens are unusual plants. They do not have flowers and some of them do not have stems or roots. Instead of seeds, they make tiny spores that will grow into new plants.

The Fly agaric toadstool is poisonous.

Puffball spores

Puffballs pop and blow out clouds of tiny spores.

Fungi, or toadstools, are not green and do not have leaves or roots. Unlike other plants, they do not make their own food. They send tiny hairs down into rotting plants or animal dung so that they can feed on them.

Ferns grow in damp, shady places. They range in size from tiny moss-like plants to huge tree ferns. Ferns produce small, round spores underneath their leaves.

Carpets of moss grow in damp places. Close up, the moss looks like forests of tiny stems and leaves.

A fern frond slowly unfurls as it grows bigger.

Crusty lichens grow on trees, rocks and old stonework. They grow very, very slowly.

Water plants

Many different plants live in water. They grow in rivers, ponds, lakes and even in the sea. Most of them are rooted in the mud beneath the water. Some water plants are huge, while others can only be seen using a microscope.

Tall reeds grow along the edges of rivers and lakes. Water lilies grow nearer to the middle. Their stems grow up through the water and their big, flat leaves and flowers float on the surface.

Common reed

Water lily

Mangrove trees grow in saltwater swamps in hot countries. Their roots are like giant stilts. The roots hold the tree in place and keep its branches above the water.

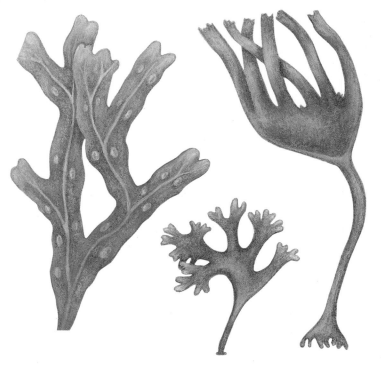

Green, red and brown seaweeds grow along rocky seashores. They do not grow in the seabed, but cling to rocks instead. Seaweeds get their food from seawater. They soak this up with their rubbery branches, called fronds.

The Amazonian water lily grows along the River Amazon in South America. Its enormous floating leaves can be up to two metres wide.

Plants and animals

Without plants, there would not be any animals. Plants provide all kinds of animals with food and homes. In return, animals help to scatter the seeds that will grow into new plants.

Harvest mouse

Harvest mice eat grass seeds, like lots of other small animals. The spiky seedheads of some plants stick to their fur and are carried to different places, where the seeds fall off and grow.

Some animals only eat one kind of food. Koalas live in eucalyptus trees in Australia. They eat nothing but the juicy eucalyptus leaves.

Goldfinches also feed on seeds. They crush them in their beaks. Some of the seeds are scattered on the ground in birds' droppings.

Leaf-cutter ants snip up leaves and carry them to their nest, where they are chewed into a pulp. The ants feed on fungus that grows on the leaves.

Plant meat-eaters

There are some very strange plants that eat meat. Insects that land on them looking for nectar find themselves caught in the plants' clever traps. Juices from the plants slowly turn the insects' bodies into liquid, and the plants soak up the liquid food.

The leaves of the sundew plant are covered in sticky hairs. When an insect lands on a leaf, it gets stuck to the hairs and cannot escape.

Venus flytrap

Sundew

The sundew leaf slowly folds over the insect to trap it.

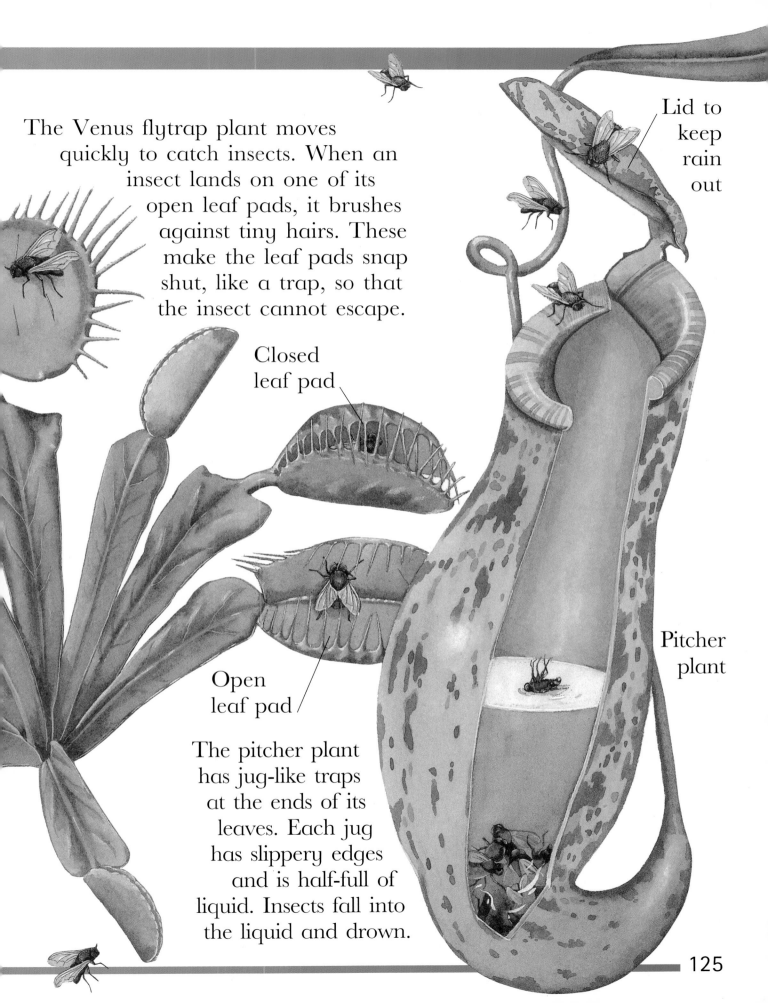

The Venus flytrap plant moves quickly to catch insects. When an insect lands on one of its open leaf pads, it brushes against tiny hairs. These make the leaf pads snap shut, like a trap, so that the insect cannot escape.

Lid to keep rain out

Closed leaf pad

Open leaf pad

Pitcher plant

The pitcher plant has jug-like traps at the ends of its leaves. Each jug has slippery edges and is half-full of liquid. Insects fall into the liquid and drown.

Plant defences

Plants are always under attack from hungry animals. They cannot run away, so they have different ways of protecting themselves. Some plants have thorns or stings. Others are poisonous or taste nasty.

If the leaves of poison ivy are damaged, milky juice leaks out of them. This juice makes the skins of animals itch and gives them painful blisters.

Cacti are juicy inside because they store water and food in their stems and leaves. They have sharp spines to protect them from thirsty desert animals.

Giraffes can stretch their necks high into trees to reach food. They like to eat the tender leaves and shoots growing on acacia trees. The acacia tree has tough, spiny thorns which stop other animals eating it.

Some nettle leaves are covered with tiny stings. If an animal brushes against the plant, its stings pierce the animal's skin and inject it with painful chemicals.

Plants called 'living stones' use camouflage to protect themselves from animals. Their leaves look like the stones around them, so that they are hard to spot.

Plants we eat

Many of the things we eat and drink are made from plants. Fruits and vegetables come from plants, and so do flour, sugar, coffee and chocolate. Nearly all plant foods are grown as crops by farmers around the world.

The vegetables we eat come from different parts of vegetable plants. Some are roots, such as carrots. Others may come from the leaves, stems, pods or seeds of plants.

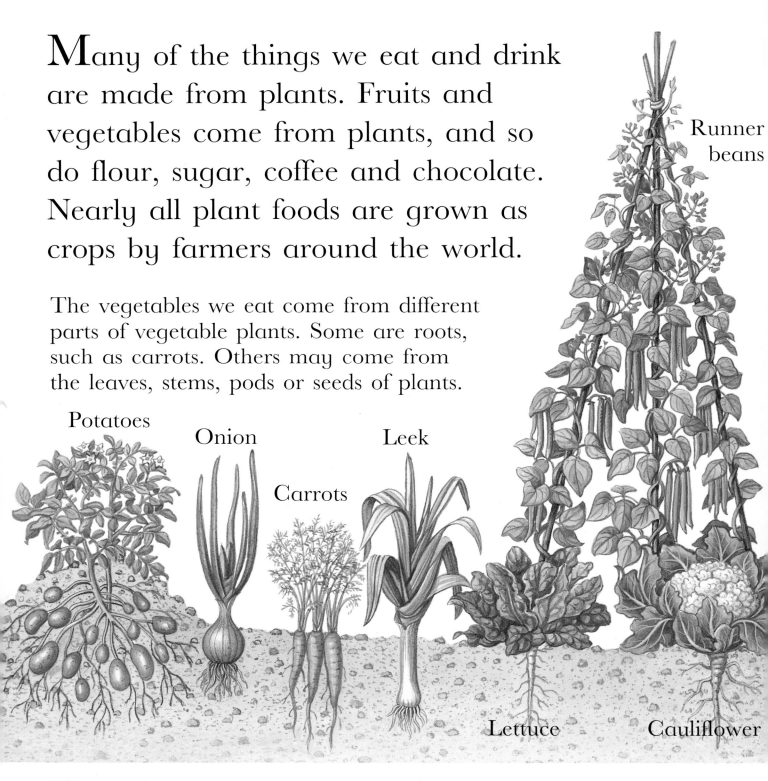

Runner beans

Potatoes

Onion

Carrots

Leek

Lettuce

Cauliflower

Grapes

Olives

Fruit grows on bushes, trees and vines. Grapes are often made into wine, and olives can be pressed to make olive oil.

Cereals are grasses grown for their seeds or grain, such as wheat, oats and rice. Many are ground into flour or made into breakfast cereals.

LETTUCES IN POTS

Fill a seed tray with compost. Sprinkle lettuce seeds on top. Spray the seeds with water and cover with a clear plastic bag. Keep the compost damp and remove the bag when tiny plants appear. Plant them in their own pots when they grow bigger.

Unusual plants

Some plants are very unusual. They might be a strange shape, have a peculiar smell or grow to an enormous size. Others look normal, but they live in places where no other plant can survive.

The rafflesia is the biggest flower in the world, measuring nearly one metre across. It smells of rotting meat to attract the flies that pollinate it.

In some deserts, flowers burst into bloom only after it has rained. They quickly make seeds, then die. The seeds sometimes lie in the ground for many years until it rains again.

Bonsai trees are tiny. They look just like normal trees, but some are only a little bit larger than a butterfly. Bonsai trees do not grow like this naturally. People trim their roots to stop them growing any bigger.

The largest and the oldest living things on Earth are the giant redwood trees of California in the United States. The tallest tree is over 112 metres high. Its trunk is more than 25 metres thick.

Giant redwood

Animal World

What is a reptile?

Snakes, lizards, crocodiles and turtles are all reptiles. They have dry, scaly skin. Reptiles are cold-blooded. This means that their bodies are the same temperature as their surroundings. They lie in the Sun to warm up, then hide in the shade to cool down.

Most reptiles hatch from eggs, like this baby snake. Reptile eggs do not have hard shells. Instead, they are soft and leathery.

Gecko

Snakes and lizards, such as this gecko, shed their skins as they grow. A new layer of skin is ready underneath.

A snake does not smell things with its nose, but with its forked tongue. It flickers its tongue in and out to track down food.

Forked tongue

The frilled lizard spreads out its neck frill to make itself look very fierce and frighten away enemies.

Frilled lizard

Snakes

There are thousands of different snakes. Most of them live in warm countries. The smallest snakes are only as long as your hand. The biggest can grow up to 10 metres long. All snakes are meat-eaters and they swallow their prey whole.

The coral snake (above) bunches itself up like a concertina, then slithers forwards. Snakes do not have legs, but they can move very fast.

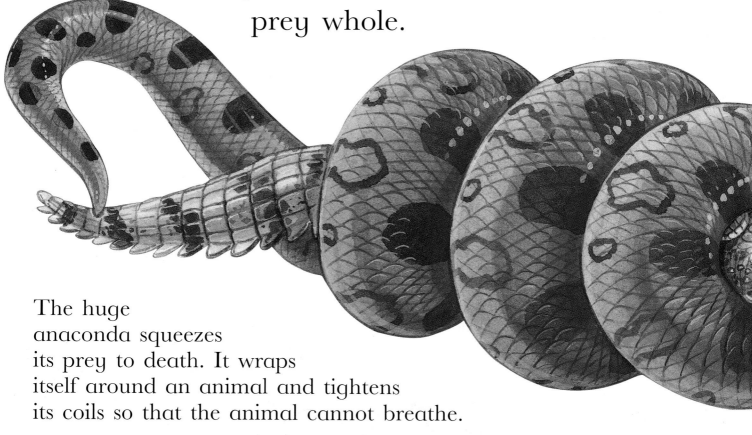

The huge anaconda squeezes its prey to death. It wraps itself around an animal and tightens its coils so that the animal cannot breathe.

Tree snakes live high in the treetops of rainforests. They coil their bodies around branches and lie in wait for tasty small animals.

Some snakes are poisonous. Rattlesnakes sink their fangs into their victims and inject them with deadly poison.

Caiman

SNAKES ALIVE!

Draw a large spiral on a piece of paper. Colour patterns on it and draw two eyes in the centre. Cut the snake out along the spiral and hang it from a piece of thread.

Lizards

Geckos, iguanas, skinks and chameleons are all lizards. They usually live on the ground, but some spend their lives scuttling about in the treetops or burrowing under the ground. Most lizards eat insects.

Many lizards are brightly coloured and patterned. This eyed lizard gets its name from the blue spots along its sides.

The Gila monster is a poisonous lizard. It makes poison in its mouth and bites small animals to kill them.

138

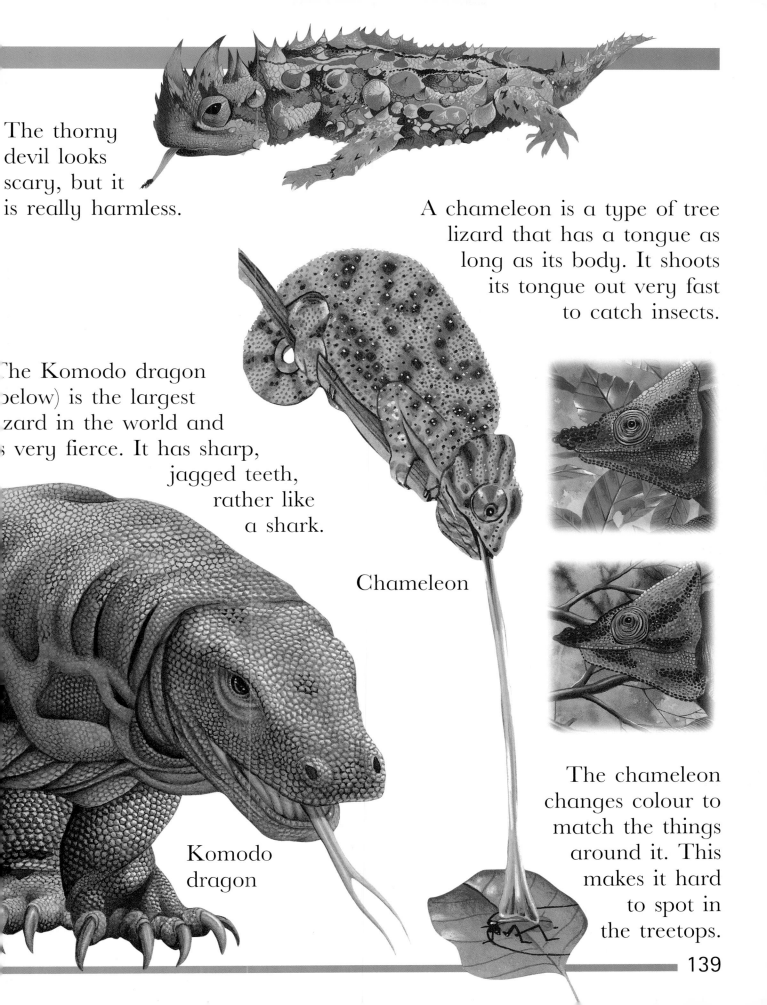

The thorny devil looks scary, but it is really harmless.

A chameleon is a type of tree lizard that has a tongue as long as its body. It shoots its tongue out very fast to catch insects.

The Komodo dragon (below) is the largest lizard in the world and is very fierce. It has sharp, jagged teeth, rather like a shark.

Chameleon

Komodo dragon

The chameleon changes colour to match the things around it. This makes it hard to spot in the treetops.

139

Turtles

Turtles and tortoises are the only reptiles with a heavy shell to protect them from enemies. Tortoises usually live on land. Turtles live in the sea and can swim quickly with their strong flippers. Turtles and tortoises both lay their eggs on land.

2. The turtle digs a hole. She lays her eggs in it and covers them with sand.

1. A turtle swims to a sandy beach at night to lay her eggs.

3. When the baby turtles hatch, they climb out of the sand and run to the sea.

A tortoise moves very slowly. When something scares it, it tucks its head and legs right inside its shell.

Giant tortoises live on the Galapagos Islands. They may live for up to 50 years and grow to be one metre long.

Crocodiles

Crocodiles usually live in rivers in hot countries. They spend most of their time lying in the water, waiting for animals to come to drink. Then they lunge forward to attack. Few animals can escape their sharp teeth.

Crocodiles float with their eyes and nose above the surface.

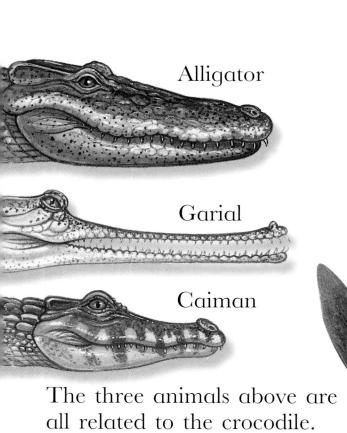

Alligator

Garial

Caiman

The three animals above are all related to the crocodile. Each one has a different snout.

An alligator (above) lies on a sunny riverbank to warm up. It cools down by wallowing in deep pools of water.

A mother crocodile (below) looks after her eggs. When they hatch, she carries the babies gently down to the river in her huge mouth.

Amphibians

Most amphibians are born in water, but live on land when they are adults. Frogs, toads, salamanders, newts and caecilians are all amphibians. They eat insects, snails and other small animals.

Frogs have smooth, slimy skin and long back legs. They are good at jumping and swimming.

Great crested newt

Newts spend part of the year on land. They usually sleep all through the cold winter. In the spring they find a pond to lay their eggs.

144

Toads are chubbier than frogs and have dry, lumpy skin. They have shorter legs than frogs and waddle about quite slowly.

Like newts, salamanders have long tails. They are shy animals that hide in damp places under logs or rocks.

The caecilian looks like a worm, but it has sharp teeth. It lives in tropical rainforests and burrows in the leaf litter on the ground.

Frogs

Frogs live in many different places. Some can even be found high up in the treetops. All frogs lay their eggs in water. The tiny creatures that hatch do not look like frogs at first, but they change as they grow. This is called metamorphosis.

A frog can leap a long way because its back legs are like springs. It starts with them folded To jump, it unfolds its long back legs and springs forwards.

1. A frog lays hundreds of eggs. The eggs are laid in clear jelly. They are called frogspawn.

Mother frog

2. Tadpoles grow inside the eggs.

Tree frogs have sticky pads on their fingers and toes to help them grip on to branches.

FROG LEAPS

See if you can jump like a frog. Squat down and put your hands on the floor between your feet. Take a giant leap forwards and land in the same position. Why not have a frog race with your friends?

3. The eggs hatch into tadpoles.

5. The tadpoles turn into frogs and leave the water.

4. The tadpoles grow bigger and develop legs.

What is a fish?

Fish live in water and are amazing swimmers. Some fish are as small as tadpoles and others longer than crocodiles. Some are flat and others tube-shaped. But most fish have the same basic features.

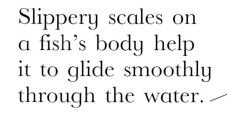

Slippery scales on a fish's body help it to glide smoothly through the water.

Most fish lay eggs. They lay hundreds of tiny eggs at a time.

Fish use their fins to steer and turn as they swim.

A fish does not have any eyelids, so it always swims with its eyes wide open.

Some fish live in the sea, where the water is salty. Others live in rivers and lakes. These are called freshwater fish.

Fish have slits called gills on the sides of their heads so that they can breathe underwater.

A fish swims along by beating its tail from side to side.

AN AQUARIUM

Paint the inside of a box blue-green. Turn the box on its side and put pebbles and shells inside it. Draw, colour and cut out pretty fish. Tape a string to each fish and tape them to the top of the box.

Coral fish

Thousands of brightly coloured fish dart through the clear blue waters around a coral reef. Corals grow in many shapes and colours, like a rocky garden under the sea. The water is shallow and sunny, and there is plenty to eat.

Most of the fish that live on coral reefs have colourful spots or stripes. This makes it hard for a hunter to spot them swimming through the corals.

1. Trumpet fish
2. Cowfish
3. Parrot fish
4. Butterfly fish
5. Lion fish
6. Angel fish

Sea hunters

Many of the creatures that live in the sea feed on plants, but others are fierce and deadly hunters. Some sea hunters rely on speed to catch their prey, but others have more unusual ways of finding their food.

The great white shark hunts by scent. When the shark smells food, it charges towards it with amazing speed. The shark snaps its prey up in its huge jaws and swallows it whole.

152

The whale shark is the biggest fish in the world, but it only feeds on the tiniest sea creatures, called plankton.

An octopus slithers along the seabed and grabs shellfish with one of its eight long arms.

The Portuguese man-of-war trails its long, stinging tentacles through the water to catch fish.

Octopus

153

Deep-sea fish

In the deepest parts of the sea the water is pitch-dark and freezing cold. No plants grow and there is hardly any food, but some very strange creatures still manage to live there.

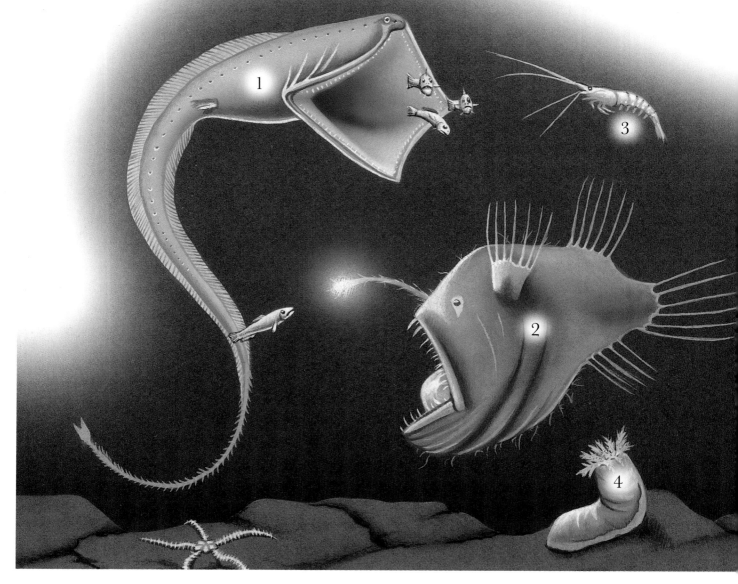

Many of the fish that live in the deepest part of the sea are black, so they are very hard to see. Some of them have tiny lights on their bodies. These attract smaller fish, which make tasty food. The lights also act as a signal to help them to find a mate.

1. Gulper eel
2. Angler fish
3. Deep sea shrimp
4. Sea cucumber
5. Flashlight fish
6. Tripod fish
7. Brittle star

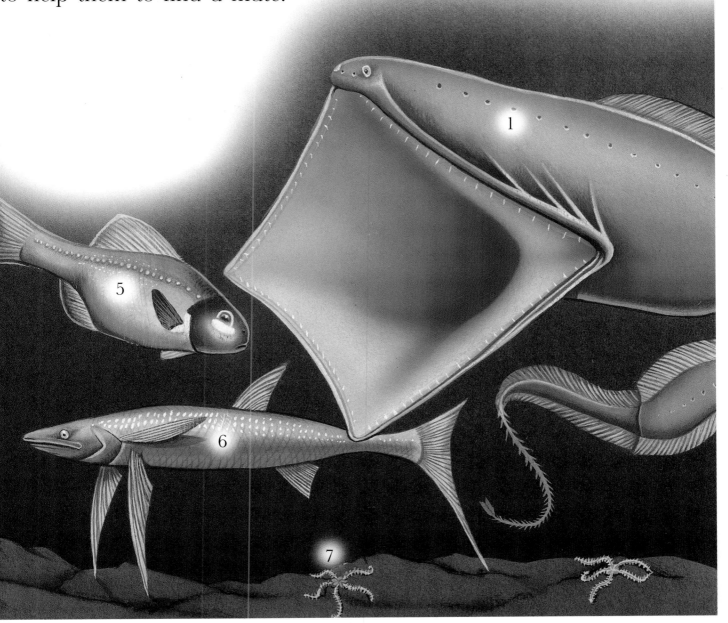

Life in a shell

Many of the animals that live along the seashore or on the seabed have shells to protect their soft bodies. These creatures can be all shapes and sizes, from giant crabs to tiny shrimps, almost too small to see.

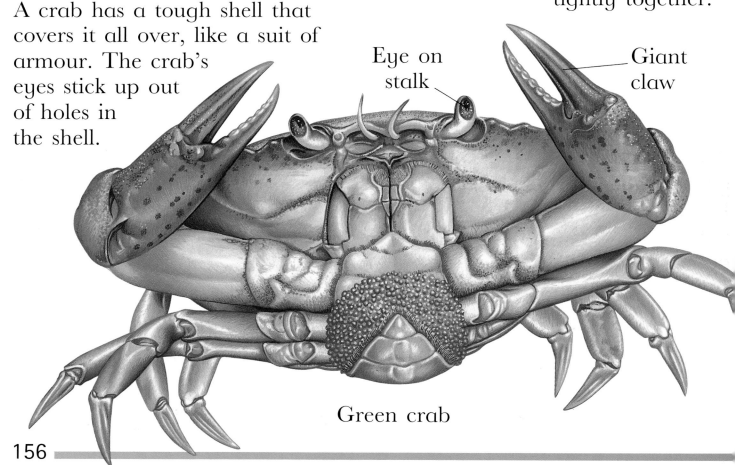

Mussels have two shells that shut tightly together.

A crab has a tough shell that covers it all over, like a suit of armour. The crab's eyes stick up out of holes in the shell.

Eye on stalk

Giant claw

Green crab

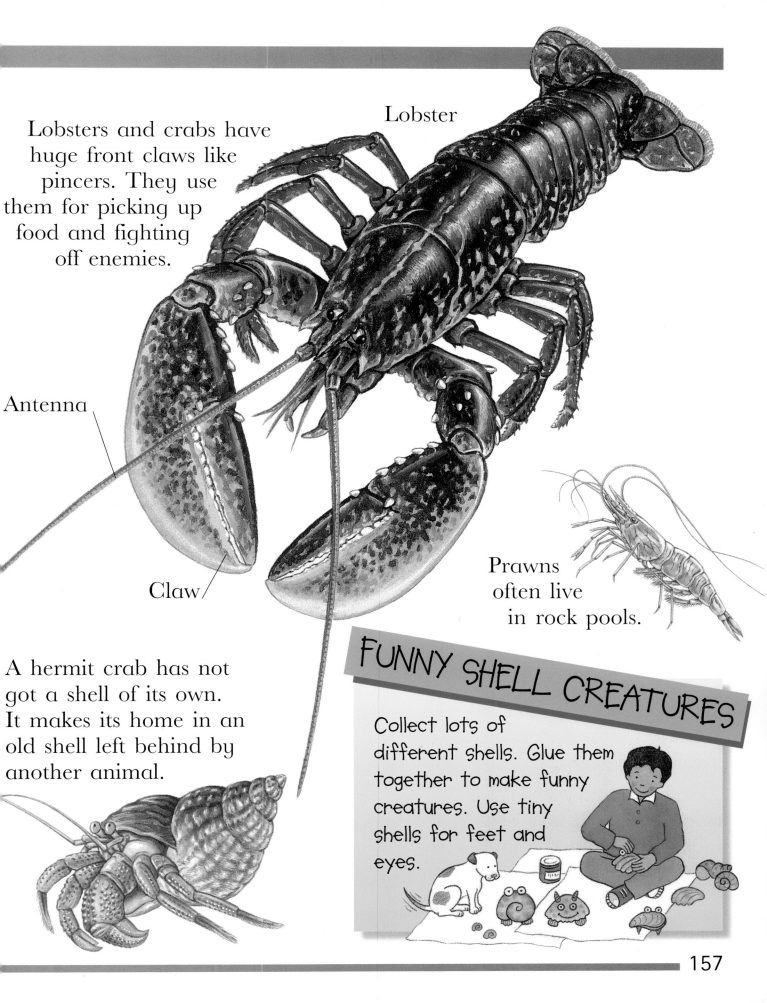

Lobsters and crabs have huge front claws like pincers. They use them for picking up food and fighting off enemies.

Lobster

Antenna

Claw

Prawns often live in rock pools.

A hermit crab has not got a shell of its own. It makes its home in an old shell left behind by another animal.

FUNNY SHELL CREATURES

Collect lots of different shells. Glue them together to make funny creatures. Use tiny shells for feet and eyes.

What is an insect?

Most insects are small. Their bodies are made up of three parts – a head, a thorax (middle), and an abdomen (back part). An insect has six legs and two antennae. Its body is protected by a hard outer case.

Thorax

Head

Antennae

Proboscis

The wings of the brightly coloured shield bug are hidden beneath the large stripy shield on its back.

Honey bees feed on nectar, a sweet juice inside flowers. They suck up the nectar through a feeding tube called a proboscis. Honey bees also collect flower pollen.

Ants live in colonies.

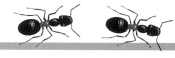

Wing

Abdomen

A butterfly has four
wings. It folds them
above its back
when resting.

This leaf insect looks
just like the leaf it is
sitting on. It is very
hard for hungry
animals to spot.

Tiny clawed leg

A stick insect
looks like
a twig.

Termites live in huge groups
called colonies. Their giant
nests, made of mud and
sand, protect the queen
termite in the centre.

Termite

Butterflies

On a warm summer's day, butterflies flutter from flower to flower, feeding on nectar. The beautiful patterns on a butterfly's wings are made of thousands of brightly coloured overlapping scales. Moths are like butterflies, but fly at night.

Monarch butterfly

A butterfly begins life as a wriggly caterpillar. It has to change completely before it becomes a butterfly.

1. A butterfly lays its eggs on a plant.

2. The eggs hatch into caterpillars.

3. The caterpillars eat and grow bigger.

Tiger moth

Moths have fatter bodies than butterflies and their antennae are not as thick as butterfly antennae. Moth antennae are feathery or look like hairs.

The death's head moth has a shape like a skull on the back of its head.

Cinnabar moth

4. Each caterpillar turns into a pupa.

5. A butterfly breaks out of the pupa.

Minibeasts

There are many tiny creatures that are not insects and cannot fly. Most of them hide away among plants or stones during the day. They usually come out to look for food at night, or just after it has rained.

An earthworm eats the soil as it wriggles its way through. It has no eyes, ears or legs.

Sting

Scorpions usually live in hot countries. They are very fierce. A scorpion catches prey in its giant pincers and kills it with the poisonous sting at the end of its tail.

Pincer

The hairy tarantula is one of the biggest spiders in the world.

A centipede has lots of tiny legs. There is one pair of legs on each segment of its body.

HAIRY SPIDER

Make a pompom by winding wool around two card discs with holes in. Push four pipe cleaners through the holes. Cut round the edge of the card and tie some wool round the middle. Take out the card. Bend the pipe cleaners to make legs, and stick on eyes.

Snails slither along the ground, leaving trails of slime behind them. If they are scared, they quickly draw back into their shells.

163

Birds and Mammals

What is a bird?

There are thousands of different birds of every colour, shape and size. Birds are the only animals that have feathers, and most birds can fly. The smallest bird is no bigger than a butterfly. The largest is taller than a man.

The tiny wren is only about as long as your finger.

A bird's body is a clever flying machine. Birds have very light bones and strong wing muscles to make it easier to fly. Their feathers keep them warm and dry. A bird's tail helps it to steer and brake when it is flying.

The shape of a bird's beak shows what kind of food it eats. The toucan's giant bill is good for plucking fruit.

The ostrich cannot fly. It is the biggest and heaviest bird of all.

The peregrine's smooth shape helps it to fly and dive very fast.

Flying

Birds are amazing acrobats. They can swoop, glide and hover in the air. Bats and insects fly too, but birds can fly faster, higher and further. Some of them are so good at flying that they can stay in the air for years.

A bird flaps its wings up and down to fly. Big birds flap their wings slowly. Small birds flap theirs fast.

Flight feathers are very smooth.

Kingfisher

Soft, downy feathers keep the body warm.

Different birds have different shaped wings, to suit the way they live. A kingfisher has short, stubby wings. Strong wings like this help the kingfisher to get back into the air from water after diving.

Contour feathers give the body a streamlined shape.

168

A goose lifts its wings right up above its back.

Then it pulls its wings down again.

The albatross glides through the skies on huge wings over three metres across. The wings are narrow and the same shape as a glider's.

Tiny hummingbirds hover while they suck nectar from flowers. They beat their wings very fast – 50 to 80 times a second. This makes a loud humming sound.

MAKE A FLYING DUCK

Draw the outline of a duck on thick card. Colour in both sides and cut it out. Draw and cut out   two wings with tabs, as shown. Fold the wings along the dotted lines. Glue the wings to the duck. Hang it from a piece of thin elastic.

Birds of prey

Birds of prey are fierce hunters with sharp beaks and claws, and very good eyesight. They soar high in the sky, hunting for small animals or fish. When they spot an animal moving beneath them, they drop down from the sky and kill it.

Eagles are the biggest birds of prey. They have long, sharp claws called talons, and they attack feet-first. The bald eagle catches fish. It swoops down to the water, grabs a fish and carries it away.

Owls hunt at night and can see well even in the dark. Fringed feathers at the edges of their wings help them to fly without a sound.

Groups of vultures gather at a kill. Vultures are scavengers. They usually eat animals that are already dead.

BEAKY BIRD CARD

Fold some card in half and cut a slit in the middle. Fold back the corners and push them inside out. Glue the card to more card, leaving the beak free. Draw a bird's face round the beak. Now open and close the card.

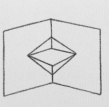

Water birds

Many birds live near water. Some of them are good at swimming and some just wade at the water's edge. Seabirds feed on fish from the sea. Other birds nest close to rivers or lakes, where there is also plenty of food.

Ducks, geese, swans and most seabirds have webbed feet. These help them to swim quickly.

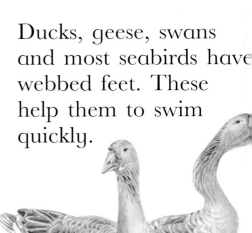

Puffins dive into the sea to catch fish. Their colourful beaks are so big that they can hold several small fish at a time. Huge groups of puffins make their nests on steep cliffs.

The heron has long legs like stilts and a sharp beak like a dagger. It stands very still at the edge of a river or lake, waiting for fish. When the heron spots one, it stabs it with its beak and gulps it down.

The Arctic tern travels further than any other bird. It nests near the North Pole, then flies to the South Pole at the other end of the world for the winter. In the spring, it flies all the way back to the North Pole again.

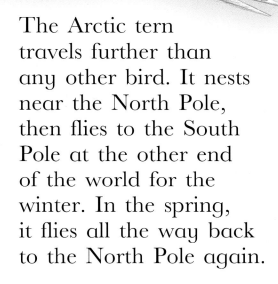

Penguins fish in the icy cold seas near the South Pole. They have short wings like flippers and swim so fast that they look as if they are flying through the water.

Nests and eggs

All birds lay eggs that hatch into chicks. Most birds make soft nests in which to lay their eggs. They build them in safe places, away from enemies. Then the birds sit on their eggs to keep them warm until they hatch.

When a chick is ready to hatch, it uses a special tooth to chip a hole in its eggshell. When the hole is big enough, the chick pushes its way out, head first.

Crows build big, untidy nests high in treetops. The nests are made of sticks bound together with mud and moss. Inside, they are lined with a thick layer of soft wool or hair.

The chicks squawk for food.

174

The Indian tailor bird makes its nest by sewing leaves together with silk from a spider's web.

Swallows build cup-shaped mud nests high up on walls, out of reach of enemies.

The chicks are covered in fluffy down.

The plover does not make a nest. Instead, it lays its eggs on shingle, where the speckled eggs are well camouflaged.

Mammals

Mammals are animals whose bodies are covered with fur or hair. They feed their babies on milk. There are many different mammals. Most of them live on land, but some of them live in the sea.

Like many mammals, pigs give birth to several babies at a time. The piglets push and shove to take turns at drinking their mother's milk.

White-sided dolphin

Dolphins and whales are mammals that live in the sea. They cannot breathe underwater, so they come up to the surface to breathe.

Bats are the only mammals that can fly. They come out to hunt for food at night and roost during the day. Bats have furry bodies and leathery wings that stretch along their arm and finger bones.

A rabbit has a thick furry coat, like many mammals. Its fur keeps it warm and dry and protects it from injury. A rabbit can see, hear and smell very well. These sharp senses help it to look out for enemies.

177

Apes and monkeys

Apes, monkeys and humans all belong to a group of animals called primates. The easiest way to tell an ape from a monkey is to look for a tail – a monkey has one, but an ape does not. Gorillas are the largest apes of all.

Gorillas are shy, gentle creatures. They live in family groups and like playing together.

Howler monkeys make one of the loudest animal sounds.

Orang-utans live alone, but they care for their babies just like humans.

MONKEY CHAIN

Trace the monkey shape above several times on to thick card and cut out the shapes. Hook the arms and tails of the monkeys together into a chain.

Hunting

Many mammals are meat-eaters. This means that they have to catch other animals to eat. Animal hunters are armed with sharp teeth and claws, and can usually run very fast. Some animals hunt alone. Others work together to track down their prey.

Wolves and other wild dogs hunt in groups called packs. Each pack has a strong dog as a leader. The wolves work as a team to catch large animals.

The cheetah can run faster than any other animal. It silently slinks as close as it can to its prey, then sprints forwards and takes it by surprise.

Bears kill other animals with a swipe of their massive paws. The brown bear likes fish. It hooks salmon out of the water as they swim upstream to lay their eggs.

Living in a herd

Animals that eat plants spend most of their time grazing on grass or munching leaves. Many of them live on grasslands where there is nowhere to hide from hunters. Here it is safer for them to live together in large herds.

Wild horses move from place to place in herds. Each herd is made up of female horses and their foals. They are led by a stallion, a male horse.

Mother elephants and their babies live together in family groups, led by an older female. All the adults help to look after the babies.

Wildebeest live in enormous herds. Each herd travels great distances, looking for fresh grass to eat.

MAKE AN ELEPHANT CHAIN

Fold a long piece of paper into wide pleats. Draw an elephant on the top fold, with its trunk and tail touching each side, as shown. Cut out the elephant and open the paper out to make an elephant chain.

Rodents

Rodents are mammals with big, sharp front teeth. They use them for gnawing and chewing things. Some rodents eat grasses, roots and tough seeds. Others will eat anything that they can find.

A squirrel often perches on the same spot to eat. It holds nuts or tree seeds in its front paws and cracks them open with its strong teeth.

Rats live in large groups called colonies. They live near canals, on rubbish dumps, in old buildings and even in people's homes. Rats eat anything. They will chew their way through wires, walls, wood and plastic.

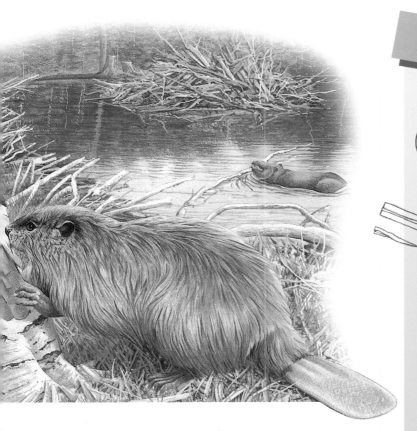

Make two card ears. Find two black beads and three paper ties. Twist the ties as shown. Draw a nose and mouth on the finger of a glove with a pen. Glue ears to the back. Sew on beads as eyes and ties as whiskers.

Beavers are amazing builders. They gnaw around trees to make them fall down and use the wood to dam a stream. Then they build a home out of branches and twigs in the middle of the pond they have made.

Marmots are furry rodents that live high in mountains. Large family groups live in burrows under the ground. In winter, they block the entrances to their burrows and sleep until spring.

185

Marsupials

Marsupials are mammals with a pouch where their babies grow. The babies are tiny when they are born. They crawl up into their mother's pouch and live there until they are bigger.

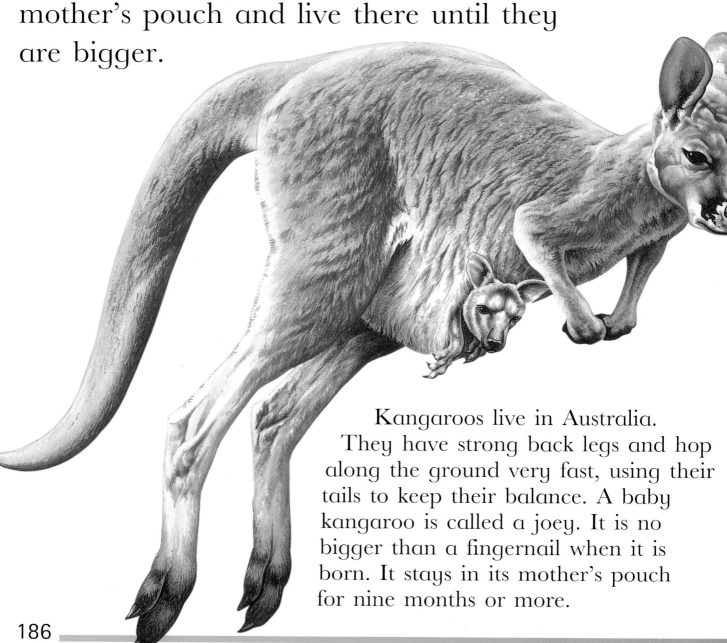

Kangaroos live in Australia. They have strong back legs and hop along the ground very fast, using their tails to keep their balance. A baby kangaroo is called a joey. It is no bigger than a fingernail when it is born. It stays in its mother's pouch for nine months or more.

Koalas are not bears. They are related to opossums. Koalas live in eucalyptus trees in Australia. Eucalyptus leaves are the only thing they eat. The leaves are so juicy that koalas never need to drink.

Opossums live in trees. Baby opossums live for 10 weeks in their mother's pouch, then they climb out and cling tightly to her fur.

ROO PENCIL POUCH

Draw a big kangaroo outline on felt and cut it out. Cut out two ears and a pouch. Glue the ears to the roo and sew on the pouch. Draw a face and arms. Glue on beads for eyes.

Water mammals

Some mammals spend most of their time in water. All water mammals are very good swimmers. Many of them dive deep underwater to catch fish. They can stay there for a long time, but they must return to the surface to breathe.

Otters live by rivers and seas. They have thick waterproof fur to keep them warm when they swim in cold water.

Hippotamuses live in Africa. During the day they wallow in rivers and lakes to keep cool. At night they go ashore to find grass and plants to eat.

The blue whale is the biggest animal in the world. It eats tiny shrimps called krill. It sieves them out of the water through a bony fringe in its mouth called a baleen.

Seals live in cold seas. They have a thick layer of fat called blubber to help keep them warm. Seals have flippers instead of back legs. They are fast swimmers and chase after fish, squid and octopus.

Strange mammals

From the tiniest mouse to the biggest whale, mammals come in every shape and size and some of them are very strange indeed.

The armadillo curls up when it is in danger. Its body is protected by bony plates of armour.

The aardvark lives on African grasslands. It eats insects called termites. When it finds a termite mound, it rips it open with its sharp claws and licks up the insects with its long, sticky tongue.

INVENT AN ANIMAL

The giraffe has long legs and a very long neck. It can stretch right up into the trees, to pull off juicy leaves and shoots that other animals cannot reach.

Fold a long piece of paper into sections, as shown below. With a friend, take it in turns to draw part of a different animal on each section. When you open the paper out, you will see the animal you have invented!

The platypus is furry. But it also has a flat beak and webbed feet, like a duck. It is the only mammal that lays eggs.

Animals in dange

Sadly, some animals are in danger of dying out forever. Thousands of animals die every year because their homes are destroyed when forests are chopped down. Other animals are killed by hunters.

Great auks are extinct now. 'Extinct' means that an animal has died out. Great auks were hunted for food until there were none left.

Tigers were in danger of dying out in India a few years ago, so a campaign was launched to save them. Special wildlife parks were set up where tigers could live safely.

The giant panda is one of the rarest animals in the world. There are fewer than 1,000 of them left. Pandas live in lonely parts of China. They only eat bamboo. Every few years the bamboo dies off. Some pandas die because they cannot find enough food.

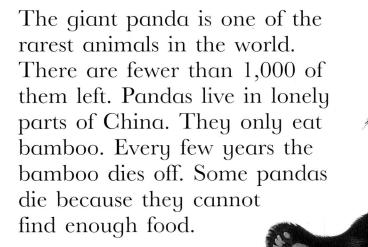

The black rhinoceros lives in Africa and feeds on leaves and twigs. For a long time hunters have killed rhinos for their horns, which are used to make Asian medicines. Now it is against the law to hunt rhinos.

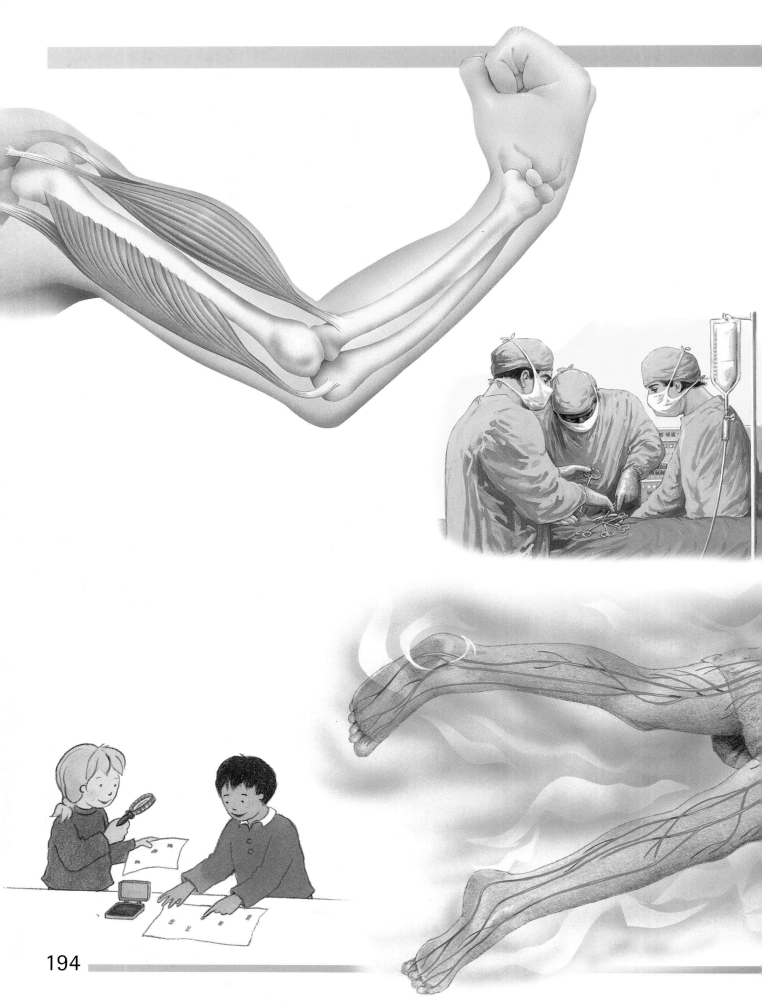

Your Body

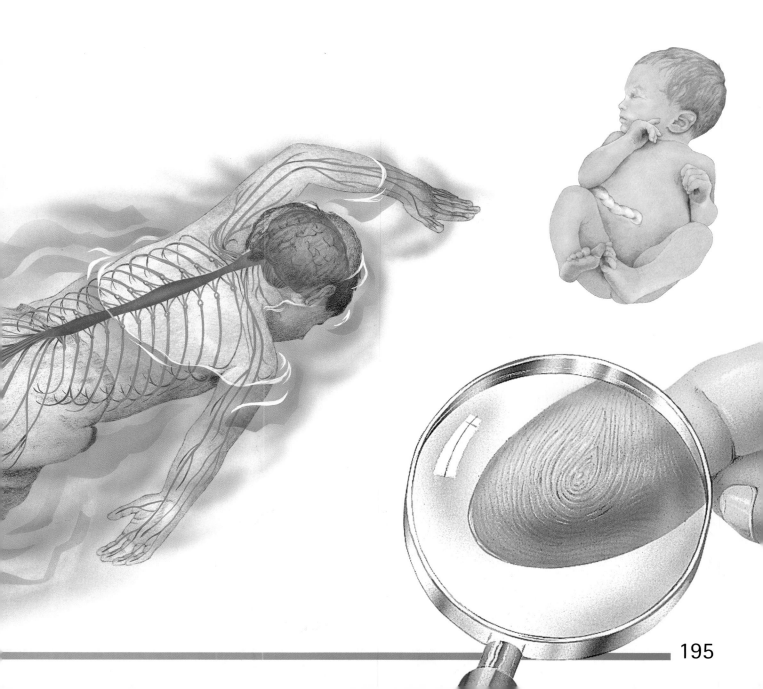

Different people

There are millions of people in the world, and they are all different shapes, sizes and colours. But underneath their skin, everyone's body is made up of the same parts and works in the same way.

Think about all the people that you know. No two are exactly the same. Out of all the people in the world, there is no one exactly like you.

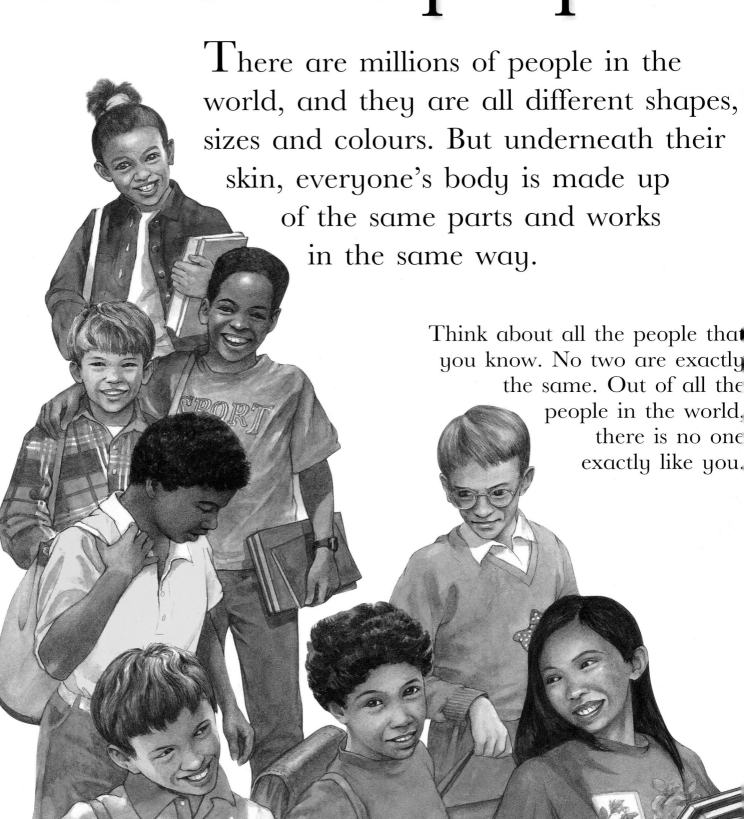

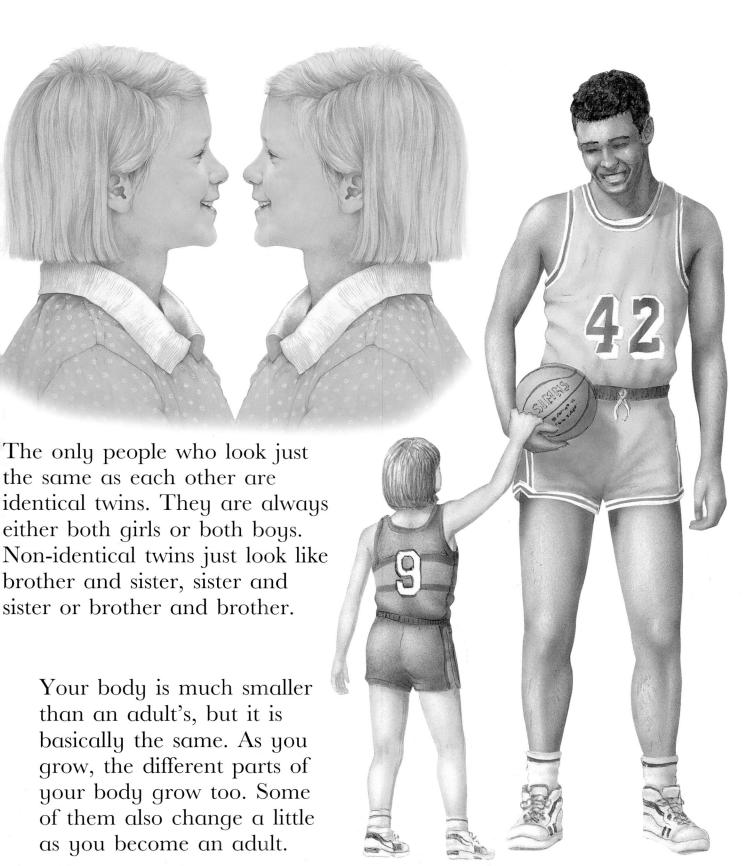

The only people who look just the same as each other are identical twins. They are always either both girls or both boys. Non-identical twins just look like brother and sister, sister and sister or brother and brother.

Your body is much smaller than an adult's, but it is basically the same. As you grow, the different parts of your body grow too. Some of them also change a little as you become an adult.

Inside you

Inside your body there are soft parts called organs that are hard at work all the time. Each organ has a special job to do to keep your body working properly. They all work together like the different parts of a machine.

Your brain, lungs, heart, liver, stomach and intestines are organs. They receive all the things they need from your blood, as it flows around your body.

Brain

Lungs

Heart

Liver

Stomach

Intestines

Your heart pumps your blood around every part of your body. It beats about 70 times a minute all the time you are alive.

Lay two fingers gently on the inside of your other wrist, below the creases. Count how many beats you feel in 15 seconds. Multiply this by four to find out how often your heart beats in a minute.

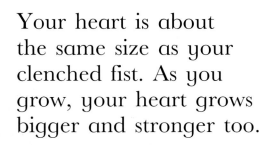

Your heart is about the same size as your clenched fist. As you grow, your heart grows bigger and stronger too.

199

Bones and joints

There are more than 200 bones that join together to make up your skeleton. This strong framework supports and protects the soft parts of your body. Without it, you would not be able to stand up or move about.

Bones are different shapes and sizes, depending on the job they do. Your skull forms a strong, bony case around your delicate brain. Your ribcage surrounds your chest to protect the organs inside.

Skull

Ribcage

Spine

Pelvis

The place where two bones meet is called a joint. The ends of the bones fit together or slide over each other smoothly.

Netball

Your joints allow you to perform many different activities.

Football

HALLOWEEN SKELETON

Draw a body, arms and legs like these on black card and cut them out. Make small holes with a pencil point where shown. Attach the arms and legs to the body with paper fasteners. Paint a skeleton on the body, using white paint. Hang the skeleton from a piece of thread to give your friends a fright!

Ballet

Tennis

Baseball

Bicycling

These children are bending and stretching their bodies in all sorts of sports.

Skin and hair

Your body is snugly wrapped up in your skin. Skin is a stretchy, waterproof covering that fits you like a glove. It protects your insides from dirt and germs, and helps to keep your body at the right temperature.

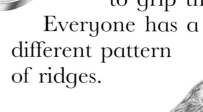

The skin on your fingertips has tiny ridges on it. These help you to grip things. Everyone has a different pattern of ridges.

Skin is not always the same colour. A brown colouring called melanin helps to protect skin from sunlight. Brown skin contains more melanin than white skin. People from hot, sunny places often have dark skin.

You are always growing new skin, because skin wears away. Hairs grow from the lower layer of your skin. Nerve endings help you to feel things. Sweat glands release sweat through tiny holes called pores. This cools you down.

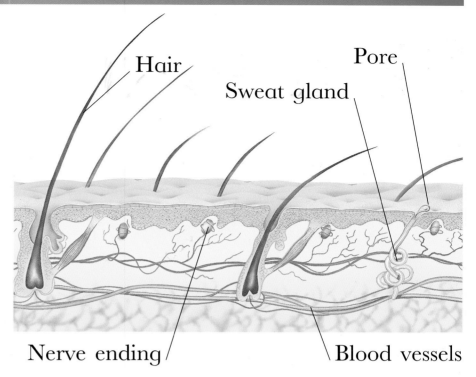

Hair
Sweat gland
Pore
Nerve ending
Blood vessels

When you are cold, you look pale because the blood vessels in your skin narrow to stop you losing more heat. Your hairs stand on end to trap body heat, and you shiver to warm up.

DETECTIVE WORK

To take a friend's fingerprints, roll each finger lightly on a stamp pad, then press it firmly on a piece of paper. Examine the prints with a magnifying glass to see the pattern on them.

The brain

Your brain is the control centre of your whole body. It keeps all the different parts working, and it never shuts down. Every time you move, your brain sends a message to part of your body, telling it what to do. You also use your brain to think and feel.

Your nerves are like a system of wires that run from your brain all around your body. They carry millions of messages between your brain and the rest of your body.

Nerves carry messages at very high speeds, so that you can react quickly to whatever is happening around you.

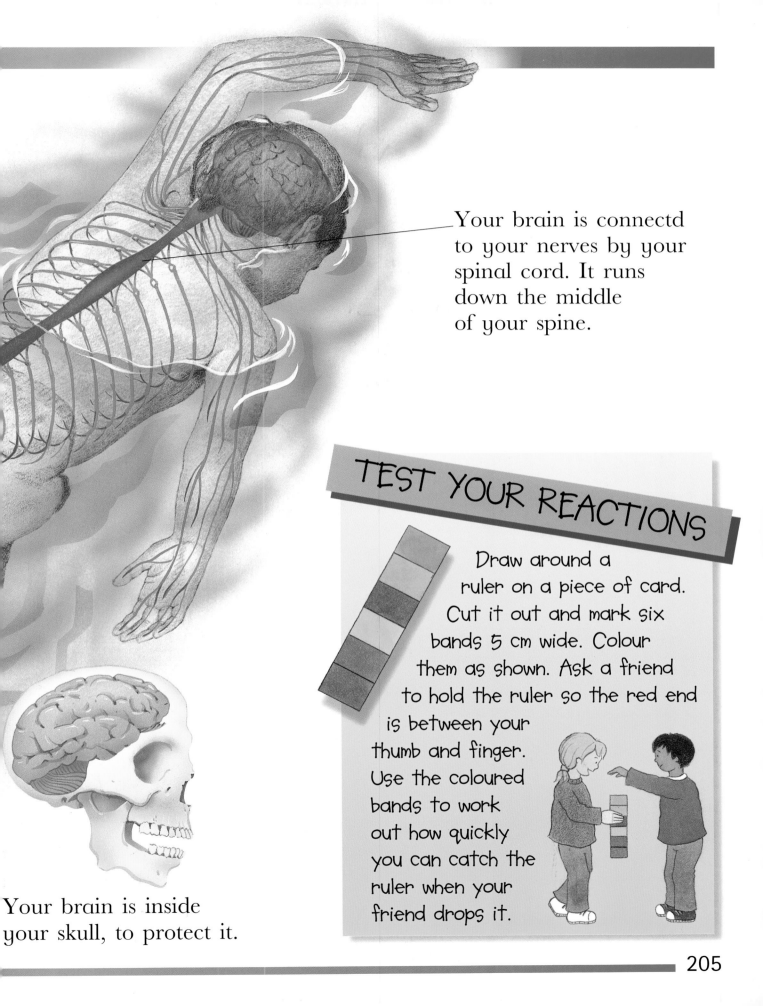

Your brain is connectd
to your nerves by your
spinal cord. It runs
down the middle
of your spine.

TEST YOUR REACTIONS

Draw around a
ruler on a piece of card.
Cut it out and mark six
bands 5 cm wide. Colour
them as shown. Ask a friend
to hold the ruler so the red end
is between your
thumb and finger.
Use the coloured
bands to work
out how quickly
you can catch the
ruler when your
friend drops it.

Your brain is inside
your skull, to protect it.

Muscles

You have more than 600 muscles that help you to move every part of your body. Every time you jump, chew or just blink, you use different muscles. The brain controls all the muscles in your body, even when you are asleep.

Tendon

This muscle tightens to bend your arm.

This muscle tightens to straighten your arm.

Muscles are joined to bones by cords of tissue, called tendons. Muscles tighten to move bones. They only pull, so they usually work in pairs.

This gymnast is using hundreds of different muscles. She exercises to make her muscles stronger so she can bend, stretch and jump more easily.

FUNNY FACE TRICKS

Some of the tiny muscles in your face are very hard to use. Have a competition with your friends to see who can waggle their ears, flare their nostrils or arch their eyebrows – without moving any other part of their face at the same time.

Muscles in your face are hard at work all the time. Tiny muscles in your eyelids tighten to make you blink and wash your eyes with tear fluid. You do this about 20,000 times a day!

Breathing

You breathe all the time, even when you are asleep. The air that you breathe into your lungs contains a gas called oxygen, which you need to stay alive. Your lungs take oxygen from the air, then your blood carries it all the way around your body.

Windpipe

Lungs

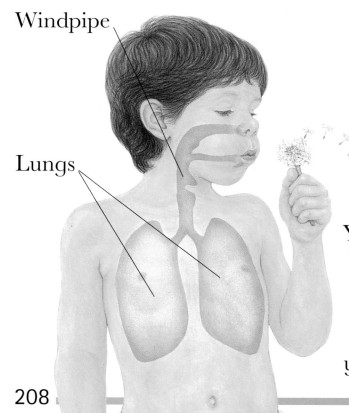

Your lungs are like big sponges. When you breathe in, they fill with air. When you breathe out or blow, they push out a waste gas called carbon dioxide that your body doesn't need.

208

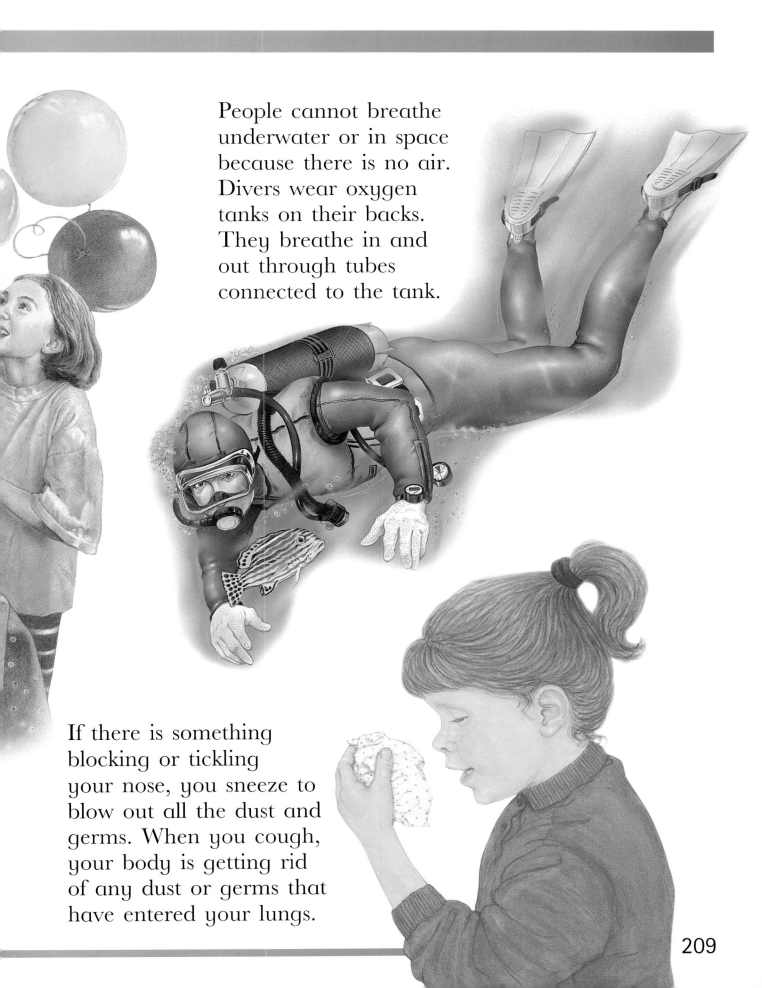

People cannot breathe underwater or in space because there is no air. Divers wear oxygen tanks on their backs. They breathe in and out through tubes connected to the tank.

If there is something blocking or tickling your nose, you sneeze to blow out all the dust and germs. When you cough, your body is getting rid of any dust or germs that have entered your lungs.

The senses

You use your eyes, ears, nose, skin and tongue to find out all about the world around you. You look around and you listen, smell, touch and taste things. You are using your five senses.

You feel things with your skin. The skin on fingertips is very sensitive. People who cannot see, 'read' special raised text, called braille, with their fingertips.

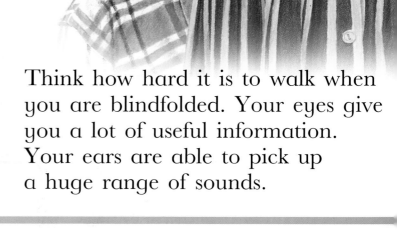

Think how hard it is to walk when you are blindfolded. Your eyes give you a lot of useful information. Your ears are able to pick up a huge range of sounds.

You taste things with your tongue, but your nose helps as well. It is hard to taste something properly unless you can smell it too.

Smells float about in the air and are picked up by your nose when you breathe in. You can tell the difference between thousands of different smells. Some things smell nice and others smell very nasty.

Your mouth

You use your mouth to eat and to speak. Your teeth chop up your food and your tongue helps you to swallow it. When you speak or sing, your lips, tongue and teeth shape the sounds you make.

The teeth you grew as a baby are called milk teeth. When you are about six, your milk teeth start to fall out. Bigger teeth grow in their place.

The surface of your tongue is covered with tiny bumps called taste buds. The taste buds on the back, sides and tip of your tongue all pick up different kinds of taste.

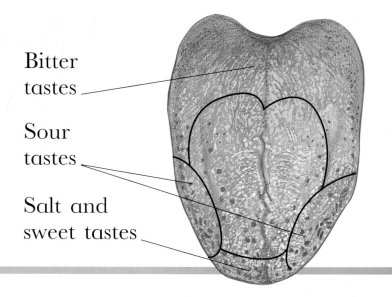

Bitter tastes

Sour tastes

Salt and sweet tastes

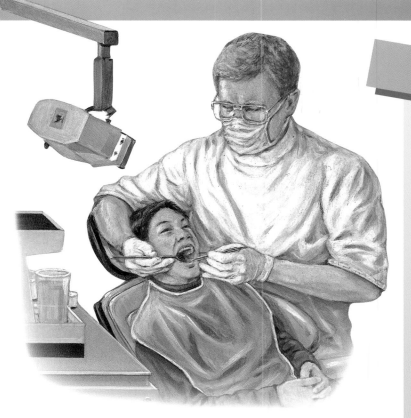

Ask an adult to hard-boil an egg. Put it in a glass and cover it with vinegar. Leave if for two days, then see how much of the eggshell has been eaten away by the vinegar. This is what sweets and fizzy drinks do to your teeth.

Dentists help you to look after your teeth. When you visit a dentist, they check that your teeth are healthy and growing properly. They also repair decaying teeth.

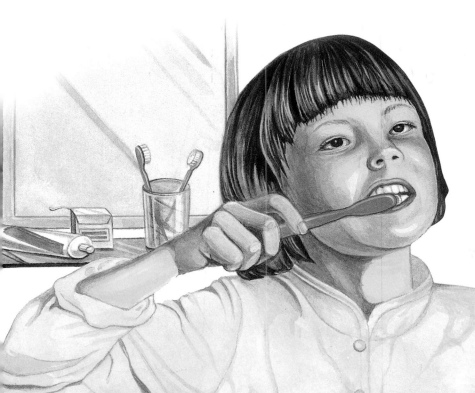

You need to brush your teeth regularly to keep them healthy. If you do not, bits of food and germs build up on your teeth to form an acid mixture called plaque. Plaque eats away at your teeth and gives you toothache.

Eating

The food you eat should give you all you need to live and grow. You need to eat many different kinds of food to stay strong and healthy, because they contain the different things that are important for your body.

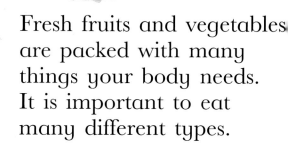

Fresh fruits and vegetables are packed with many things your body needs. It is important to eat many different types.

Your body takes all the energy you need to work and play from your food. This is why you need to eat regular meals throughout the day.

Draw a chart like this on a big piece of paper. Then write down what you eat at each meal every day for a week. How many different types of food do you eat?

Monday			
Tuesday			
Wednesday			
Thursday			
Friday			
Saturday			
Sunday			

Gullet

Stomach

Small intestine

Large intestine

After you swallow food, it travels down your gullet to your stomach. It is mixed up into a mushy soup, then it moves along your intestine. All the useful bits of food filter through the wall of your intestines into your blood.

Babies

You started life no bigger than a dot in your mother's tummy. You lived there for nine months, slowly growing until you looked like the baby shown here. Then, on your birth day, you were born and came out into a new world.

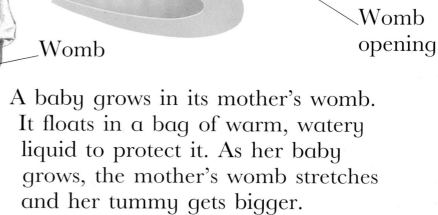

Womb

Womb opening

A baby grows in its mother's womb. It floats in a bag of warm, watery liquid to protect it. As her baby grows, the mother's womb stretches and her tummy gets bigger.

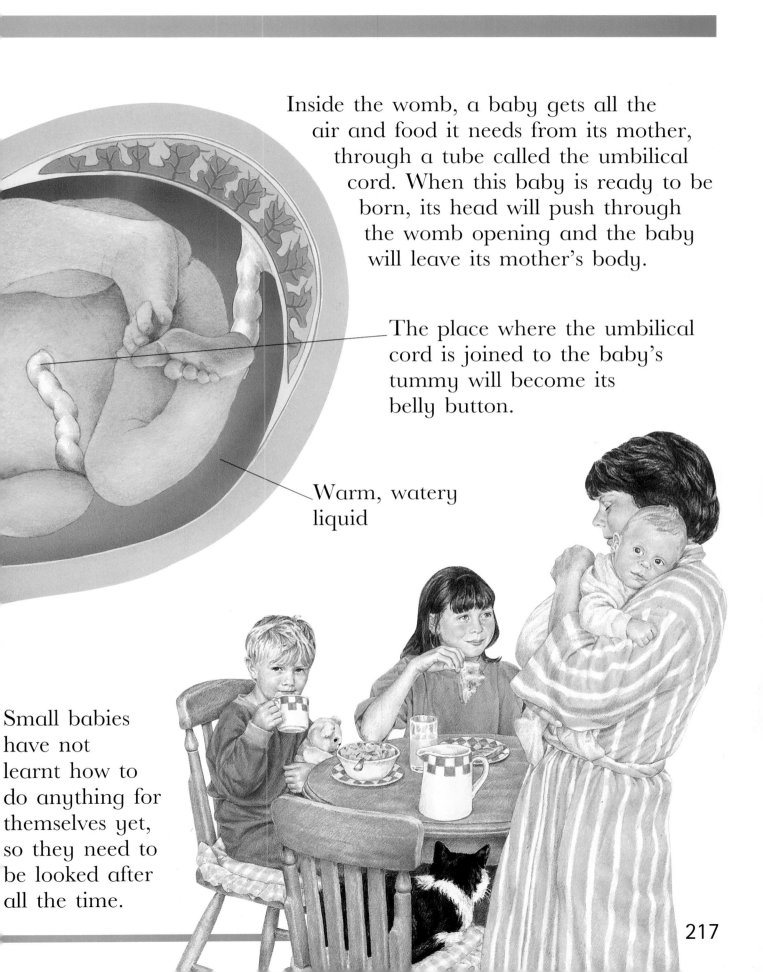

Inside the womb, a baby gets all the air and food it needs from its mother, through a tube called the umbilical cord. When this baby is ready to be born, its head will push through the womb opening and the baby will leave its mother's body.

The place where the umbilical cord is joined to the baby's tummy will become its belly button.

Warm, watery liquid

Small babies have not learnt how to do anything for themselves yet, so they need to be looked after all the time.

Growing up

All through your life, your body is changing. Babies grow into children. Before long they become teenagers, then adults. They may work and have children of their own. As children grow up, they learn the skills they will need later in life.

Children are very quick to learn. Small children learn by playing. Older children go to school. They learn to read and write, and to do sums. They find out all about the world around them. They also play games and make lots of new friends.

Everyone changes as they grow older.
Sometimes old people become a little
shorter than they were when they
were younger. Their hair
goes grey and their skin
becomes more wrinkled.

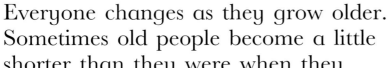

When people grow
older, they retire
and stop going out to
work. This gives them
more time for all the
things they enjoy,
such as visits from
their grandchildren.

Sleep

Everyone needs to sleep so that their bodies can recover after a busy day. When you are asleep your body works more slowly. Your breathing slows down and your muscles relax. You also dream.

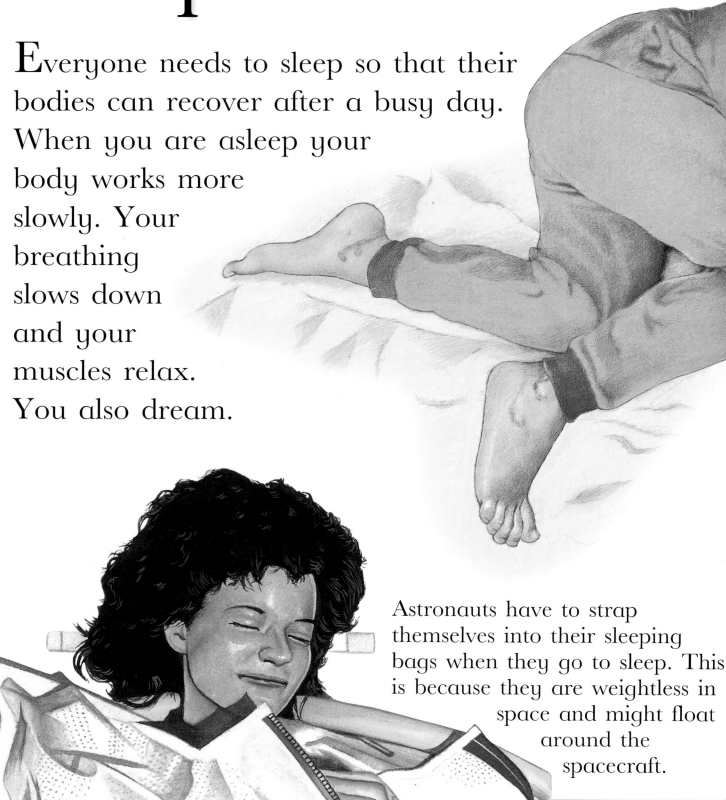

Astronauts have to strap themselves into their sleeping bags when they go to sleep. This is because they are weightless in space and might float around the spacecraft.

Babies and children need plenty of sleep because they use a lot of energy just growing. Adults have stopped growing, so they do not need as much. Most children sleep for about 12 hours a night.

Some people walk around at night while they are still asleep. This is called sleepwalking. Sleepwalkers do not remember anything about it when they wake up in the morning.

KEEP A DREAM DIARY

Dreams seem real while you are asleep, but you soon forget them. Try keeping a dream diary. Write down what happened in your dreams as soon as you wake up in the morning. Some of them will seem very strange to you. You could use them as ideas for stories or pictures.

When you are ill

Sometimes you get ill. You might have a cough, a high temperature, spots, or aches and pains. These are all signs that your body is trying to fight off an infection. Infections are caused by harmful germs too small to see.

Some illnesses, such as chicken pox, are infectious. This means that they are easy to catch. But once you have had them once, you do not usually catch them again.

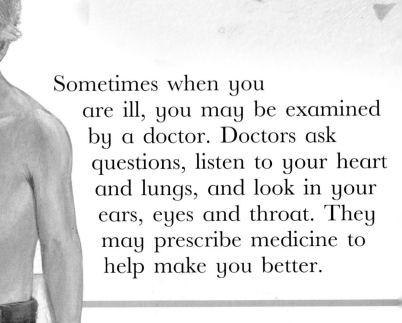

Sometimes when you are ill, you may be examined by a doctor. Doctors ask questions, listen to your heart and lungs, and look in your ears, eyes and throat. They may prescribe medicine to help make you better.

There are many tablets and medicines for different illnesses. Some medicines are given as injections. People with asthma use inhalers to help them breathe more easily.

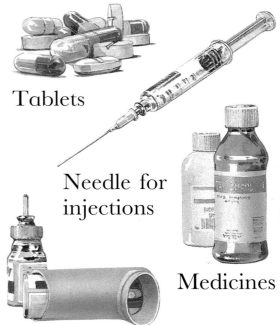

Tablets

Needle for injections

Medicines

Inhaler

If people have an accident or are very ill, they go to hospital. They may have an operation so that doctors can mend the part of the body that is damaged. They stay in hospital until they are well.

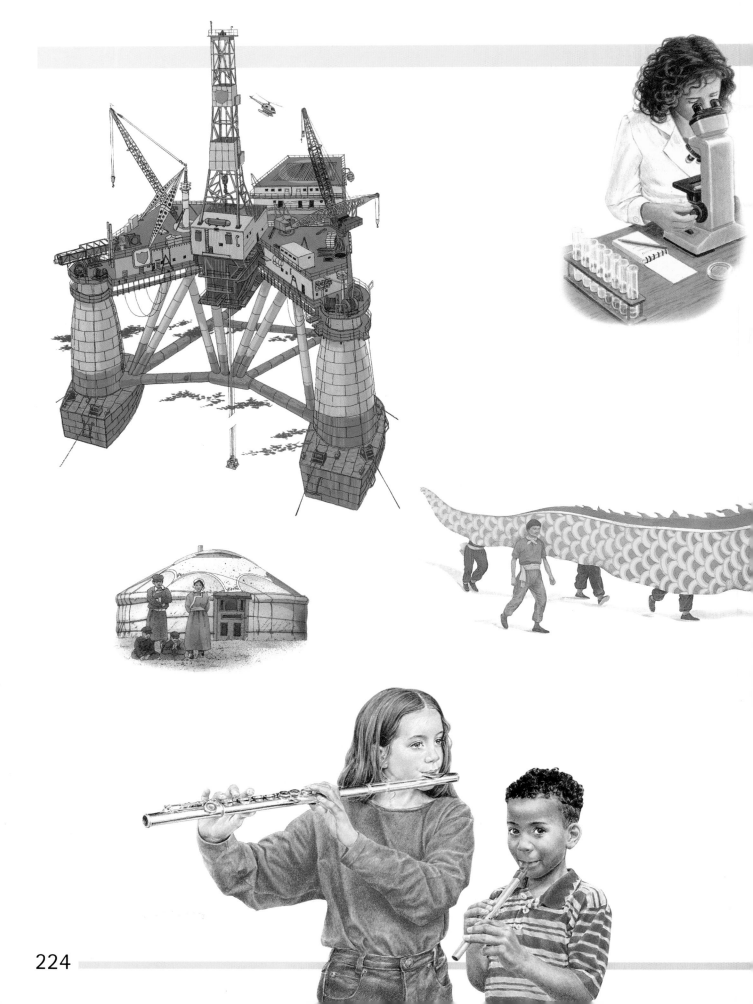

People and Places

Around the world

There are billions of people living on Earth. They live in different countries and speak many languages. People often do the same things, but they may have different customs and traditions.

These children come from all over the world. They are holding their countries' flags. Every country has its own flag, sometimes with a symbol of the country on it. A symbol is a picture or pattern that means something special to people.

Every country ha its own range of postage stamps. They often show interesting things in that country.

China

Brazil

Sweden

Greece

Germany

Israel

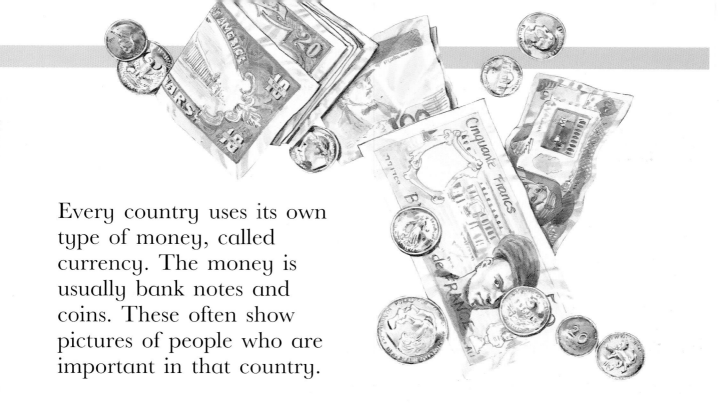

Every country uses its own type of money, called currency. The money is usually bank notes and coins. These often show pictures of people who are important in that country.

Sudan

Australia

United Kingdom

Canada

Turkey

Argentina

South Korea

Jamaica

Austria

Where you live

Whether you live in a town or in the country, there will be a map of the area. Maps show what places look like from above. The maps are much smaller than the places they show, but they tell you a lot about them.

Imagine how a bird sees a town from up in the air. Everything looks a different shape from above.

This is a map of the town from a bird's eye view. The map shows the roads, pond and buildings as shapes. Everything is drawn to scale – it is the right size compared with everything else.

MAP YOUR BEDROOM

Bedroom

Map

Draw a map of your bedroom. Pretend you are a fly on your bedroom ceiling, and draw simple shapes to show the furniture. To make everything the right size, measure your room and furniture in footsteps. Then draw your map on squared paper, pretending that each square has sides one footstep long.

Houses and homes

Around the world, people live in all kinds of different homes. They build them out of materials they find nearby. Some houses are made of bricks or stone. Others are made of wood, mud or reeds.

Some people are nomads. This means that they move from place to place. These nomads in Mongolia live in round tents called 'yurts'.

People who live near rivers and marshes often build their houses on stilts, like this house in Indonesia. It is raised high above the ground, safe from flooding.

In North Africa, some houses are built of mud, with thick walls and small windows to keep out the sun.

Tower blocks, like this one in Africa, are built in cities, where there is not much room for building. They contain many small homes called flats.

MAKE A STILT HOUSE

Cut and fold back the ends of four cardboard tubes, as shown. Tape them to the bottom of a cardboard box. Fold a piece of cardboard in half and tape it to the box to make a roof. Paint doors and windows on the box. Glue yellow drinking straws to the roof.

This house in the United States was built from bricks and wood. Both materials were easy to buy nearby.

Jobs people do

People do all kinds of different jobs. They work to earn money to buy their homes, food and clothes. Most people start work when they leave school or college.

Teachers work in schools and colleges. They teach children how to read and write, and many other things that they need to know. Some teachers teach all kinds of subjects. Others teach just one subject.

Health workers teach people how they can stay strong and healthy. This woman is holding a clinic for mothers and their babies.

Builders work in teams to build new homes, offices and other buildings. This man is a bricklayer. He is carrying the bricks with which he builds walls.

Many people work with machines that make things. This baker is in charge of a machine that makes bread, slices it and wraps it in plastic.

Industry

Industries produce things that people need. Many industries make things, such as cars or buildings. Others produce the raw materials needed to make things, such as metals or oil.

The car industry produces cars. Billions of cars are made in factories every year. Most of them are put together on conveyor belts by robots.

Oil is needed to run machinery. There is oil buried under the sea, so oil rigs are built on high platforms in the sea. They drill deep into the seabed and pump the oil up to the surface.

Robot arm

Anchors hold oil platform in place

Helicopter landing pad

Crane

Drill

Many people work together to put up buildings. They use giant machines, like this crane, to lift massive pieces of buildings into place.

Scientists study chemicals. They work out how to make medicines, plastics and many other things that people use every day.

Land and sea

Farmers and fishermen work hard to produce all the food that we eat. Some farmers grow crops, such as cereals, fruit or vegetables. Others keep animals. Fishermen catch fish and send them to fish markets to be sold.

There are thousands of sheep on a big Australian sheep farm like this. Sheep farmers rear sheep to sell for meat. They also shear the sheep – clip off their fleeces – and sell the wool.

Most rice is grown in Asia (below). Rice needs a lot of water, so it is grown in flooded fields, called paddy fields. The rice is often harvested by hand, using sharp tools called sickles.

Wheat is usually harvested by giant combine harvesters. These machines cut the wheat and separate the grain from the stalks.

Most fish are caught in huge nets pulled behind big boats called trawlers. On board the fishermen pack the fish in ice to keep them fresh.

Food

Around the world, people cook and eat many different kinds of food. Some countries have their own special meals. For example, Italy is famous for delicious pasta dishes and India for spicy curries.

France is famous for its fine cooking. Below is a French salad made with tuna, potato, egg and olives. Next to it is a stick of French bread.

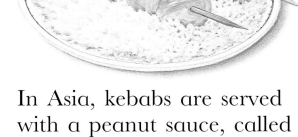

In Asia, kebabs are served with a peanut sauce, called satay.

Sushi is a traditional Japanese dish. Small pieces of raw fish are arranged on rice.

Paella is made in Spain. Rice is cooked with vegetables and chicken or fish. The rice is coloured with a yellow spice called saffron.

Chow mein is a Chinese dish. Egg noodles are fried in a big pan with chopped vegetables, and often meat or fish.

Hamburgers come from the United States. Beefburgers are served with salad in a soft bun.

FUNNY FACE PIZZA

Slice some cheese, tomatoes, mushrooms and peppers. Spread tomato sauce on a pizza base. Arrange the vegetables on the pizza base in funny face shapes. Cook in a hot oven for 10–12 minutes.

Clothes

People wear all sorts of clothes to keep themselves warm and comfortable. They put on different clothes depending on what they are doing, or whether it is hot or cold.

Children like to wear comfortable clothes that they can run around in.

People who live in cold places wear many layers of clothing to keep themselves warm. All their outdoor clothes and shoes are waterproof, to keep out rain or snow.

In India, the traditional dress for women is called a sari. It is made of a long piece of material draped round the body.

In hot countries, people often wear loose robes to keep cool. These Masai women are wearing huge beaded collars for a celebration.

These athletes are wearing special sportswear. Their clothes fit tightly and are made of stretchy material in which it is easy to move. Other sportsmen sometimes wear pads and helmets, to protect them from injuries.

241

Arts and crafts

Around the world, people make all kinds of decorative things. Some people paint pictures. Others shape pots, make jewellery or weave rugs. These skills, called crafts, are often handed down from parent to child.

The Navajo people in the United States make sand pictures on the ground for special ceremonies. The patterns are made from grains of different coloured sand. Some of the pictures are meant to show magic signs.

Many countries make fine china. The same patterns are often used again and again

242

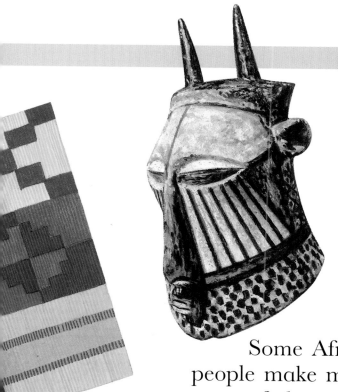

Some African people make masks out of clay, wood or metal, to wear at special ceremonies.

These brightly patterned pieces of fabric come from Ghana, in West Africa. They were woven from cotton dyed in many different colours.

In Turkmenistan, in Asia, women weave wool into colourful, patterned carpets. The country is famous for its carpets. They have been made the same way for thousands of years.

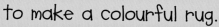

Religions

Many people around the world follow a religion. They believe in a god, or gods, who created the world and controls what happens in it. There are many religions. Each one has its own beliefs and traditions.

Hindus worship many different gods and believe that people's souls are born again after death. These women are celebrating the festival of light, Diwali. The god Shiva is shown, top left.

The religion of Jewish people is called Judaism. Jews believe in one god. They light candles in a special candlestick called a menorah during the festival of Hanukkah.

244

Muslims follow a religion called Islam, that was founded by the prophet Muhammad. They believe in a god called Allah, whom they worship in mosques. Their sacred book is called the Koran.

Minaret (tower) of a mosque

Christians worship one god and believe that Jesus Christ was his son. Their holy book is the Bible. They worship in churches, chapels and cathedrals.

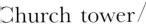

Church tower

Buddists follow the teachings of the Buddha, seen here, and worship in temples. They believe that people are born again after death and that good deeds are rewarded in the next life.

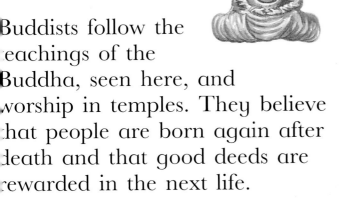

Festivals

Festivals are large celebrations with music, dancing, colourful costumes and entertainments. Most festivals mark special days or events. Many are linked to a religion, while others may just celebrate the changing seasons.

Chinese people celebrate their New Year with a festival. Huge, brightly coloured dragons lead processions through the streets. People carry lanterns and let off fireworks.

In Sweden, people decorate a maypole and dance around it to celebrate Midsummer's Eve.

During a Japanese festival called Hinamatsuri, people float paper flowers or dolls down a river to make their problems go away.

DECORATE SOME EGGS

Ask an adult to make small holes in the ends of some eggs. Blow out the insides, and rinse and dry the eggs. To paper an egg, paste small squares of paper all over it. To paint an egg, paint patterns on one half first. Let the paint dry, then paint the other half.

At Halloween, people in the United States make spooky pumpkin lanterns to scare away evil spirits.

Many Christians celebrate Easter by giving each other decorated eggs, or eggs made from chocolate.

Music and dance

All around the world people love music and dancing. They play hundreds of different musical instruments and enjoy many different kinds of music. Most countries have their own traditional music and dances.

Ballet is a graceful way of dancing that is based on set movements. Ballet dancers train for many years to learn how to perform the different steps.

This Indonesian percussion orchestra is called a gamelan. The musicians play xylophones, chimes, gongs and drums.

Music and dance play an important part in celebrations. At the festival of Esala Perahera in Sri Lanka, drummers and dancers parade next to elephants in decorative costumes.

MAKE MARACAS

Pour rice or dried lentils into an empty yogurt pot. Stand another yogurt pot upside down on top of it and tape the two edges together. Make two, decorate them, then try shaking them!

The flute and the recorder are both wind instruments. This means you blow into them. You block the holes with your fingers to make different notes.

Entertainment

There are many ways to relax and enjoy yourself. You could go out to watch a show or film, or visit a theme park. Sometimes you may prefer to read a book or play computer games.

At shadow puppet shows in Java, the audience sits either side of a screen. Half of them watch the puppets, while the other half watch the shadows on the screen.

Theme parks are very popular for exciting days out. There are many attractions, like the scary rollercoaster (below).

Towns and cities often hold big firework displays to celebrate a special occasion or time of the year. People watch as fireworks shoot into the night sky and explode in fantastic patterns and colours.

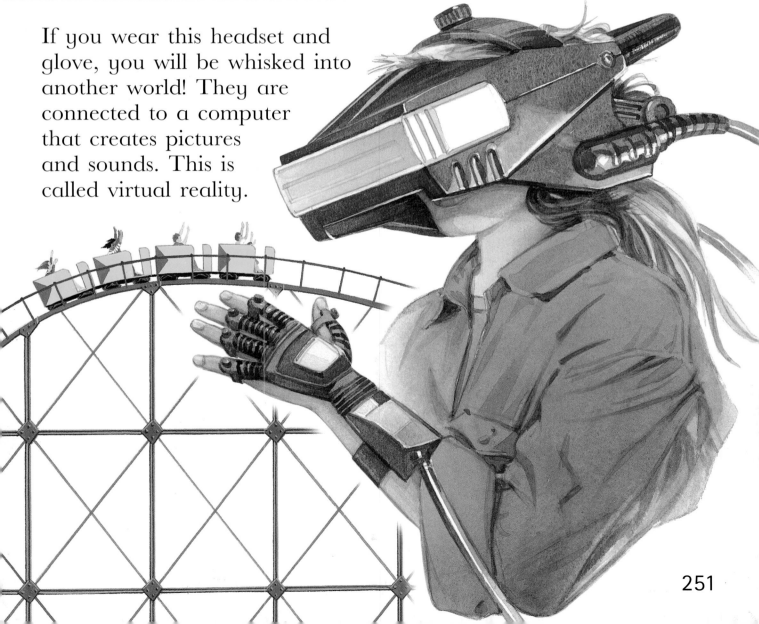

If you wear this headset and glove, you will be whisked into another world! They are connected to a computer that creates pictures and sounds. This is called virtual reality.

Sports and hobbies

Many people love sports and games. They are fun to watch and play, and they can help to keep you fit too. Many people also have hobbies. These are things they like to do in their spare time.

Ice hockey is a fast, tough game played on an ice rink. The players wear ice skates and helmets. The teams use special sticks to slide a flat disc, called a puck, into the goal.

In a game of basketball there are two teams of players. They have to drop the ball into the basket to score a goal.

Football is one of the most popular sports and it is played all over the world. Most countries have a national team that plays matches against other countries.

Chess is a board game for two players. It is like a battle. The players take it in turns to move and try to capture each other's chess pieces.

Many children have a personal computer at home. They can use it for doing their homework, exploring the Internet or playing all sorts of different games.

Transport

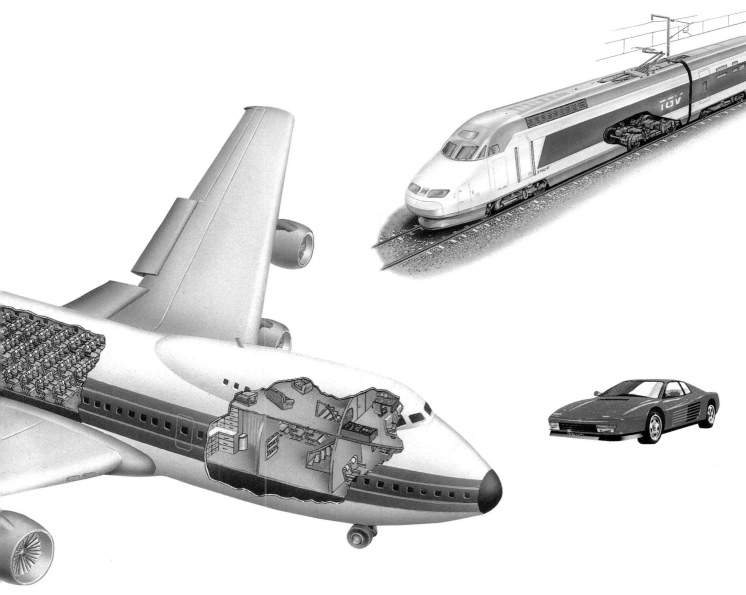

Early transport

Early cars, boats, trains and planes looked very different to the kinds of transport we use today. They were not shaped for speed like modern vehicles, and travelled much slower.

Before cars were invented, rich people travelled around in carriages pulled by horses. They were a very bumpy and uncomfortable way of getting around.

The first trains were pulled along by powerful steam engines that burned coal or wood. On the front of this train there is a 'cowcatcher' for clearing the track.

When the first aeroplanes were invented, pilots competed with each other to be the first to fly across oceans and mountains.

The first ships were made of wood. Ships like this one had many sails because they were blown along by the wind. Early explorers set off on dangerous voyages around the world in ships like this.

Early cars were much slower than modern cars. Their wheels were more like bicycle wheels than the tough rubber tyres that are used today.

Bicycles

Bicycles have two wheels. To ride a bike, you push the pedals round with your feet. This turns the chain, which makes the back wheel go round. You steer the bicycle with the handlebars. This turns the front wheel.

You can ride your bike around in town, explore the countryside or race around a cycle track. Wherever you ride, make sure that you wear protective clothing, such as a hard helmet or knee pads, to stop you getting hurt if you fall.

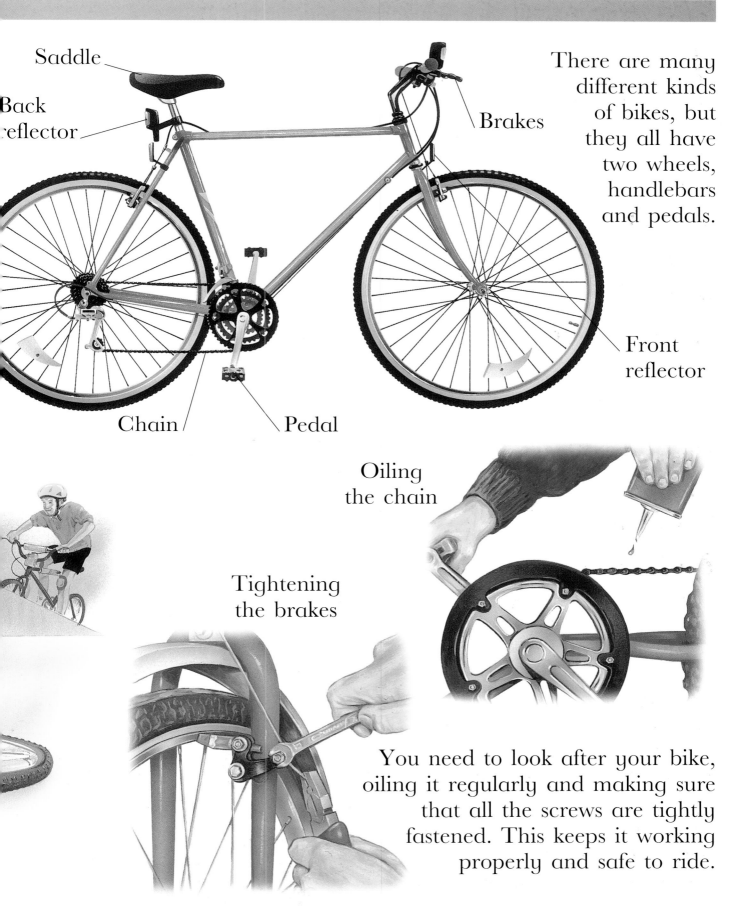

Saddle

Back reflector

Brakes

There are many different kinds of bikes, but they all have two wheels, handlebars and pedals.

Front reflector

Chain

Pedal

Oiling the chain

Tightening the brakes

You need to look after your bike, oiling it regularly and making sure that all the screws are tightly fastened. This keeps it working properly and safe to ride.

On the road

You can see all kinds of vehicles on the roads. Cars, buses and coaches take people from place to place. Lorries travel long distances, transporting all the goods that you can buy in shops.

A network of roads runs throughout every country. The largest roads that link the major cities are called motorways. In some countries, motorists drive on the right side of the road. In others, they drive on the left.

Buses and coaches can transport large numbers of people at the same time. This bus carries passengers between all the main cities in the United States.

A transporter carries new cars from the factory to showrooms around the country. The cars are fastened to the trailer, so they do not fall off the lorry as it drives along.

MAKE A FLOOR ROAD MAP

Tape several large pieces of paper or card together. Draw a road plan on them, making sure the streets are wide enough for your toy cars. Draw houses, rivers and trees and colour in the map. Lay it on the floor and drive toy cars around it.

Cars

Cars can be all sorts of shapes and sizes. People use them to go to work or to school, to go shopping or to go on holiday. Most cars have engines that run on petrol. They usually have four wheels.

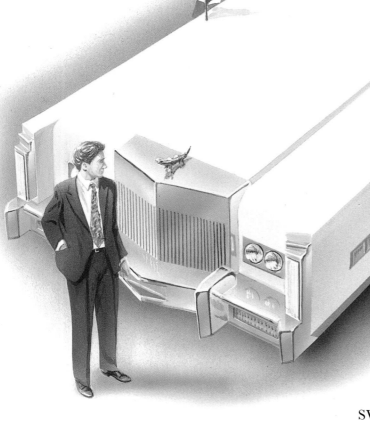

A super-stretch limousine is a very, very long car. This one is the longest car in the world. It has 26 wheels and its own luxury swimming-pool at the back.

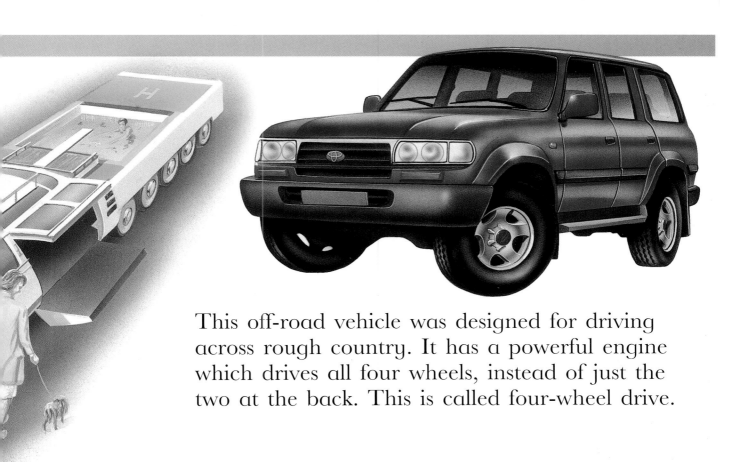

This off-road vehicle was designed for driving across rough country. It has a powerful engine which drives all four wheels, instead of just the two at the back. This is called four-wheel drive.

Sports cars are specially designed for speed. They have large engines and a smooth, flat shape that helps them to go fast. Most sports cars only have seats for two people.

Designers have been trying to invent a car that doesn't need petrol. This car has a large solar panel. It uses rays from the Sun to make energy to drive the car.

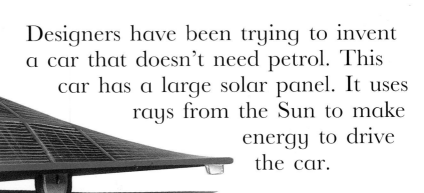

Racing vehicles

Some cars and motorcycles are built especially for racing. They are designed to go as fast as possible. Racing vehicles speed around special circuits or tracks. They are not driven on ordinary roads.

Formula One racing cars have enormously powerful engines and can drive at speeds of more than 190 kilometres an hour. Drivers compete with each other on racing circuits all around the world.

This racing car has a special 'wing' at the back. It does not work like an aeroplane's wings. Instead of lifting the car, it keeps it on the track when it is going fast.

These trial bikes are specially designed for off-road racing. They can scramble over muddy or rocky ground, and up and down steep hills.

Trucks and tractors

Trucks and tractors are working machines. They are used to pull all kinds of heavy loads, and often deliver goods across great distances. They need to be strong and sturdy and have very powerful engines.

An articulated truck pulls heavy loads on long journeys. The truck is made up of two sections so that it can bend in the middle. This helps it to go round tight corners.

Tractors are used to pull or operate many different farm machines. A tractor's giant back wheels have big, ridged tyres. These stop the tractor from slipping on muddy ground.

The truck's load is carried in the trailer.

A tanker is a type of truck. It carries all sorts of liquids, such as petrol or milk, in cylinder-shaped tanks. Some tankers have several tanks linked together.

The trailer is joined to this 'fifth wheel'.

The tractor unit has a sleeping cabin, where the driver sleeps on long journeys.

The tractor unit pulls the trailer. Its fuel is stored in huge tanks.

Diggers and dumper,

All the heavy work on building sites is done by machines. There are different machines for different jobs. Some dig holes, some lift parts of buildings and others dump huge loads of rubble.

A dump truck carries huge loads of earth and rocks, then tips them wherever they are needed. There are sliding arms called pistons underneath one end of the truck. These tip it up so that it can dump its load.

This digger is brilliant at digging holes and shifting heavy loads. It has a wide bucket at the front for moving rubble. At the back it has a massive bucket attached to a strong arm. This digs holes and scoops earth and rocks into trucks.

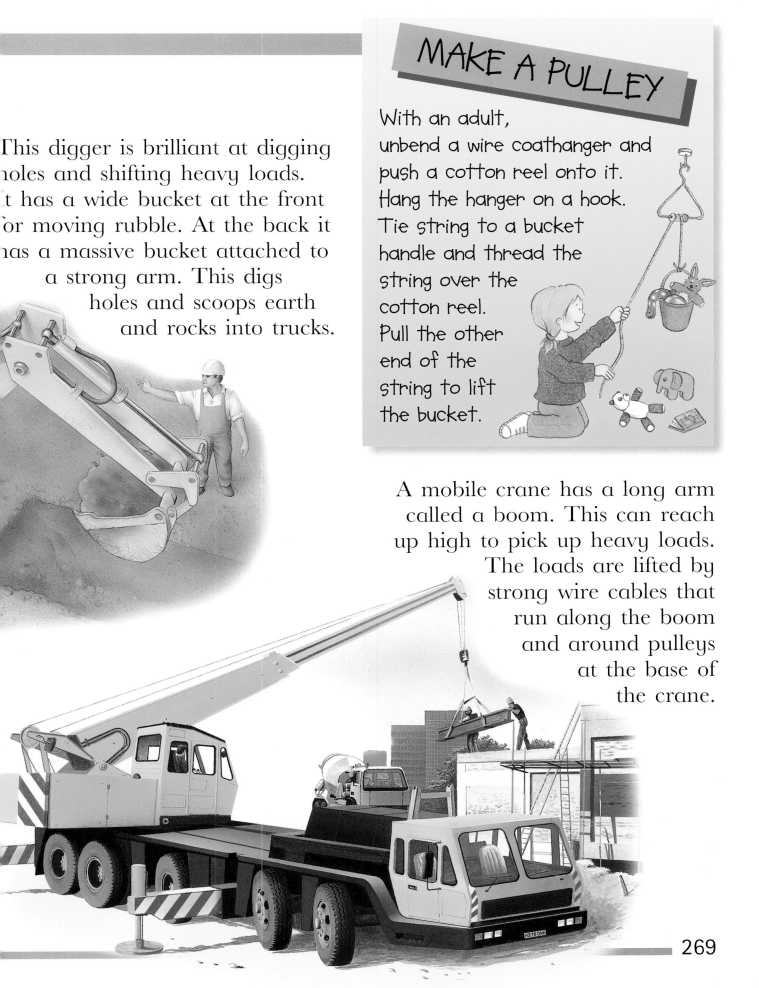

MAKE A PULLEY

With an adult, unbend a wire coathanger and push a cotton reel onto it. Hang the hanger on a hook. Tie string to a bucket handle and thread the string over the cotton reel. Pull the other end of the string to lift the bucket.

A mobile crane has a long arm called a boom. This can reach up high to pick up heavy loads. The loads are lifted by strong wire cables that run along the boom and around pulleys at the base of the crane.

Trains

Trains run on rails. They are made of carriages pulled by engines. Passenger trains carry people, and freight trains transport goods. The first trains were powered by steam, but most modern trains run on electricity or a fuel called diesel.

The Mallard recorded the fastest ever speed for steam trains. It reached a speed of 203 kilometres an hour.

The fastest passenger train in the world is the French TGV. It travels at more than 300 kilometres an hour. TGV stands for 'high speed train' in French. In this picture, you can see the insides of the train. It runs on electricity from the wires above.

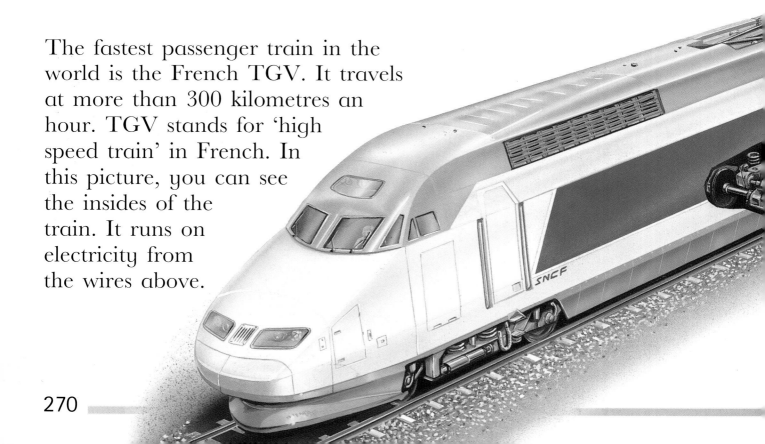

MAKE YOUR OWN TRAIN

Glue two boxes together to make an engine. Make the chimney and buffers out of cardboard tubes. Use more boxes for carriages, and paper plates for wheels.

In the United States, powerful diesel engines pull freight trains across the continent from coast to coast. The engines are strong enough to pull the carriages and their heavy cargo up mountains.

Tunnels and bridges

Tunnels and bridges make journeys shorter and easier. Bridges take roads and railways across obstacles, such as rivers and roads. Tunnels are cut through mountains and under rivers and seas.

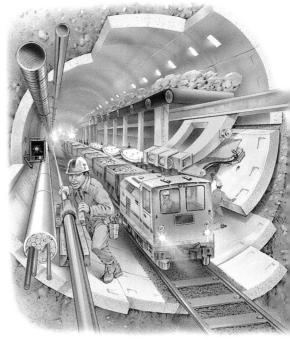

To build tunnels, people cut through the rock with giant tunnelling machines, or blast huge holes using explosives.

Underground railways are built in tunnels that run deep under the ground beneath big cities. Here you can see that different lines, going in different directions, are built at different depths.

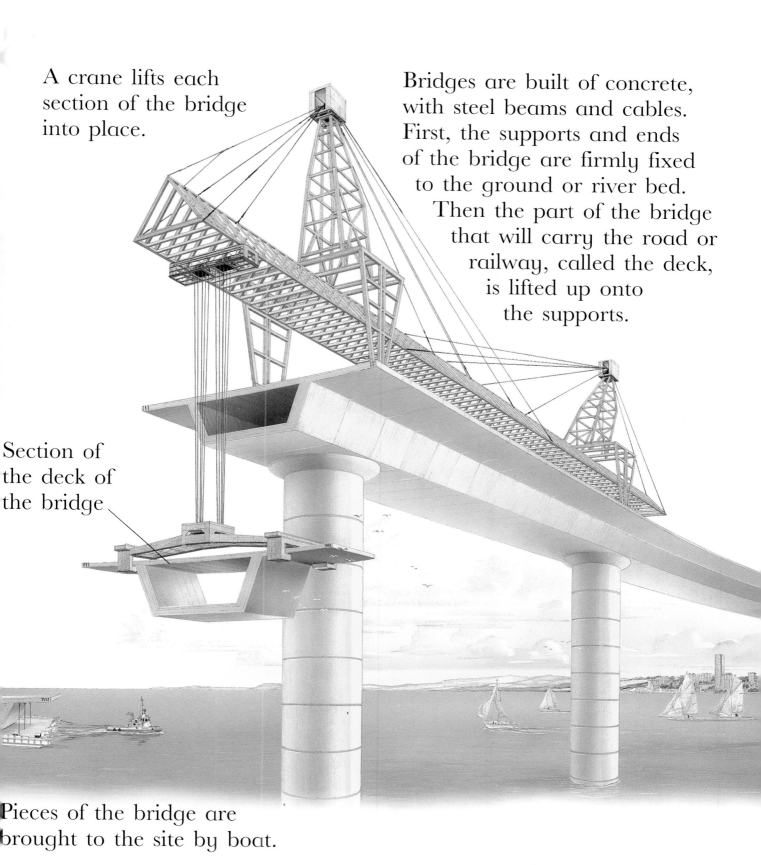

A crane lifts each section of the bridge into place.

Bridges are built of concrete, with steel beams and cables. First, the supports and ends of the bridge are firmly fixed to the ground or river bed. Then the part of the bridge that will carry the road or railway, called the deck, is lifted up onto the supports.

Section of the deck of the bridge

Pieces of the bridge are brought to the site by boat.

Ships and boats

People have built many different ships and boats to carry them along rivers and across oceans. They might want to explore new lands, or just go on holiday. Some ships carry passengers very fast, others go more slowly.

Ships like this galleon were used for early sea voyages. They were driven along by the wind, so their journeys often took months.

This is one of the first steam-powered boats. It burnt wood or coal to make steam to turn a paddle wheel at the back of the boat.

This modern ferry is a catamaran because it has two hulls. This makes it very steady in the water. It can speed along without tilting from side to side.

Hull

A slow cruise liner is like a floating hotel. There are all sorts of things to do on board. The liner carries passengers on long sea journeys, calling in at many different ports. The liner's engines drive huge propellers that go round under the water.

MAKE A CATAMARAN

Ask an adult to cut a plastic bottle in half lengthwise, to make two hulls. Stick thin strips of balsa wood across the hulls with waterproof tape to hold them together. Fill a big bowl with water and try floating your catamaran in it.

Submarines

Submarines can travel beneath the sea for many weeks without coming up to the surface. Many submarines are underwater warships that carry missiles and other dangerous weapons. Others are used to explore the depths of the sea.

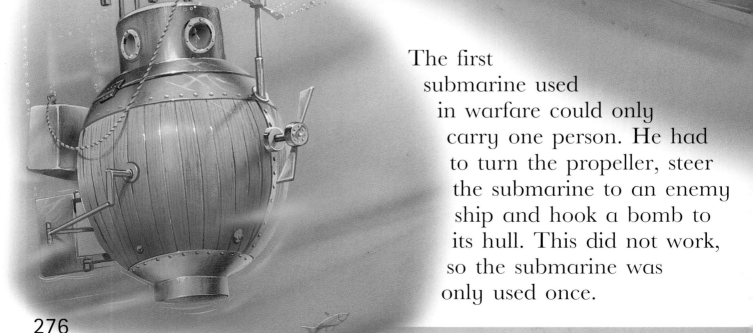

1

2

The first submarine used in warfare could only carry one person. He had to turn the propeller, steer the submarine to an enemy ship and hook a bomb to its hull. This did not work, so the submarine was only used once.

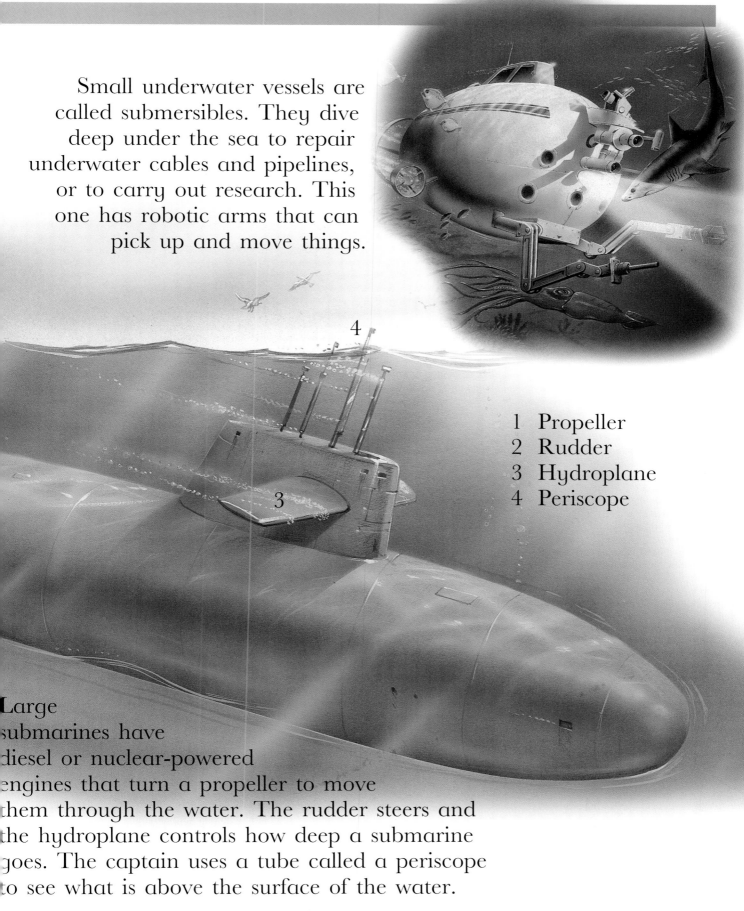

Small underwater vessels are called submersibles. They dive deep under the sea to repair underwater cables and pipelines, or to carry out research. This one has robotic arms that can pick up and move things.

1 Propeller
2 Rudder
3 Hydroplane
4 Periscope

Large submarines have diesel or nuclear-powered engines that turn a propeller to move them through the water. The rudder steers and the hydroplane controls how deep a submarine goes. The captain uses a tube called a periscope to see what is above the surface of the water.

In the air

There are many kinds of flying machine. They all fly in different ways. Some can fly very fast, others can do all sorts of tricks in the air, such as turning upside down.

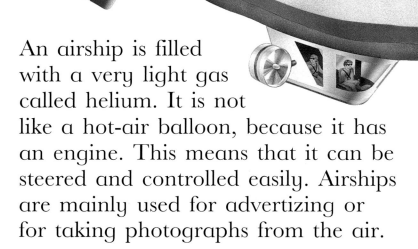

An airship is filled with a very light gas called helium. It is not like a hot-air balloon, because it has an engine. This means that it can be steered and controlled easily. Airships are mainly used for advertizing or for taking photographs from the air.

Airliners are the fastest way to travel. They carry passengers all around the world. This passenger jet can hold about 250 people.

MAKE A GYROCOPTER

Cut a piece of paper 16 cm long and 4 cm wide. Cut a slit 8 cm long down the middle. Fold the two flaps down. Attach a paperclip to the bottom of the paper. Drop the gyrocopter from a height. It will spin to the ground.

A jump jet is a fighter plane that can take off and land vertically. It rises straight off the ground without needing a runway. It can also turn very sharply and hover in mid-air like a helicopter.

A helicopter has rotor blades on its roof and its tail. These make it fly. It can go forwards, sideways and backwards, and hover in the air.

279

Travelling by air

Airliners are large aeroplanes with powerful jet engines. They can travel at speeds of more than 960 kilometres an hour. Airliners carry passengers great distances between countries very quickly.

A modern jumbo jet carries over 400 passengers. The pilot and co-pilot who fly the plane sit in the flight deck.

Fuel is stored inside the wings.

Seats where the passengers sit

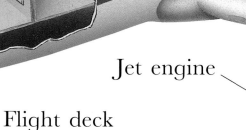

Jet engine

Flight deck

For the wing, cut out a piece of stiff paper 24 cm by 13 cm. Tape the long sides together. Cut two slits in the taped edge and fold back two flaps. Cut out another piece of paper 20 cm by 3.5 cm for the tail. Fold the middle so it sticks up. Cut off 1 cm of the flat pieces each side of the tail, and then make flaps in the flat edges. Tape the wing and tail to a drinking straw, as shown, to make your plane. Attach paper clips to the front of the straw to make it heavier. Now try flying the plane.

The tail fin helps to keep the plane steady.

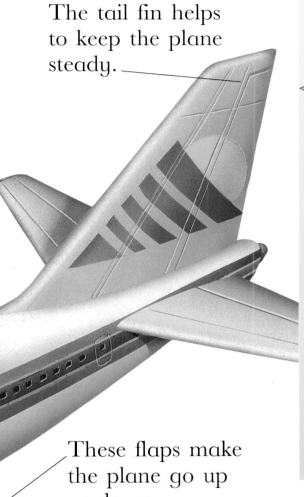

These flaps make the plane go up or down.

Flaps called ailerons make the plane turn left or right.

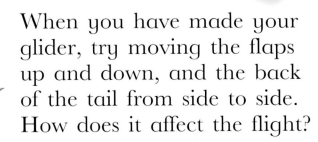

When you have made your glider, try moving the flaps up and down, and the back of the tail from side to side. How does it affect the flight?

Rescue vehicles

When there is an accident or a fire, special vehicles rush to the scene. They are specially equipped to rescue people and save buildings. The police, the fire brigade and the ambulance service are the main emergency services.

The police use fast cars or bikes with sirens and flashing lights to reach the scene quickly.

Each emergency service does a different job. Ambulances rush injured people to hospital for treatment. They have beds and medical equipment inside them. Trained staff lift people into the ambulance on stretchers and look after them until they arrive at hospital.

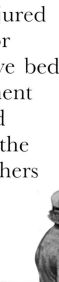

282

Fire engines have extendable ladders on turntables that reach high up buildings.

Firefighters point their powerful hoses at the flames to put out the fire.

124

How Things Work

What is science?

Science is the way we find out about the world around us. Scientists look at everything carefully so that they can understand why things happen the way they do. They learn new things all the time.

Sometimes scientists use special tools, such as this magnifying glass, to help them study things close-up.

Scientists try to answer questions about everyday things, such as "What are bubbles?" and "Why can we hear different sounds?"

Scientists ask questions about the world and guess at what the answers might be. Then they do experiments to test whether their theories were right.

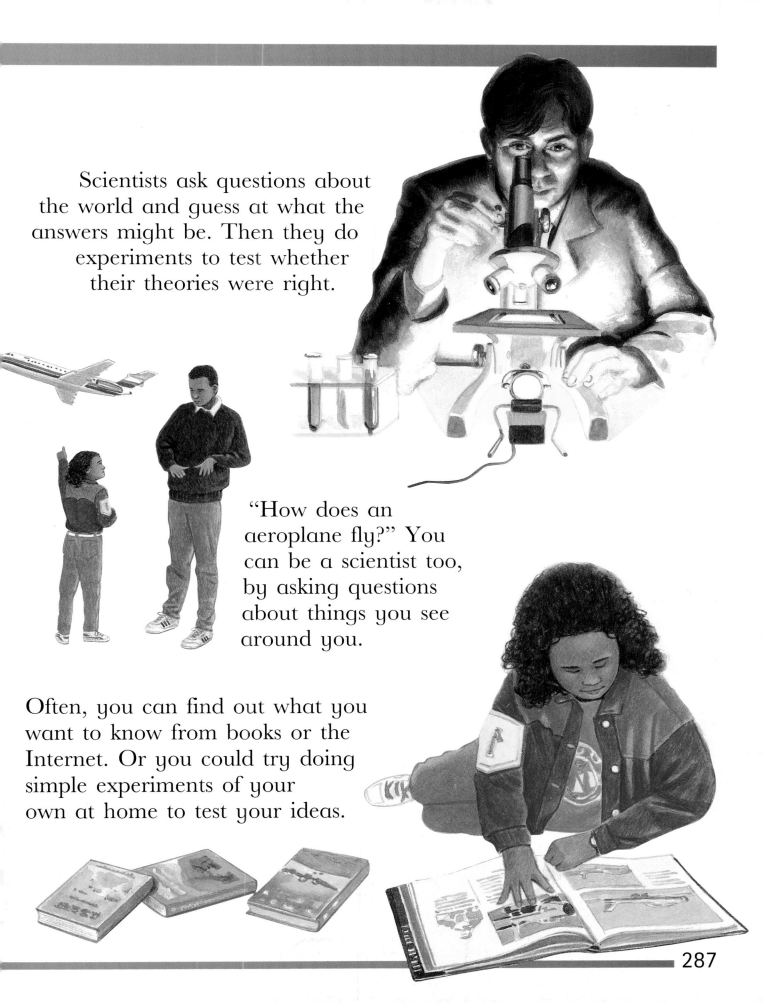

"How does an aeroplane fly?" You can be a scientist too, by asking questions about things you see around you.

Often, you can find out what you want to know from books or the Internet. Or you could try doing simple experiments of your own at home to test your ideas.

What is it made of?

The things around you are not all made out of the same material. They are made out of different materials depending on the job they have to do. Materials can be soft, hard, heavy, light, rough or smooth.

Do you know what your toys are made of? Soft things might be made of wool or fabric. Smooth things could be made of metal, plastic or glass.

Plastic

Fabric

Metal

Wool

Paper

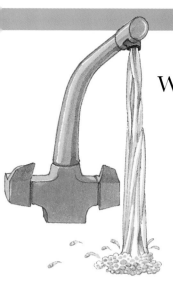

Water

Ice

Steam

Everything is either a liquid, a solid or a gas. Liquids are runny. Solids have a fixed shape. Gases spread out to fill the space they are in. Some materials can change from one thing to another. Water is liquid, but when it freezes it turns into solid ice. If water boils, some of it becomes a gas called steam.

HOMEMADE ICE LOLLIES

Pour your favourite fruit juice into some lolly moulds and put them in the freezer.

When the lollies have frozen, hold them upside down under a warm tap for a few seconds, then gently slip them out of the moulds.

Wood

Glass

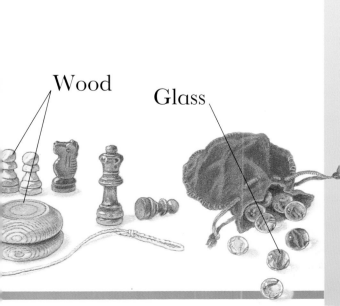

The air around us

Air is all around you, but you cannot see it, smell it or taste it. Air has no shape and spreads out to fill every space. It is a mixture of different gases. One of these is oxygen, which all animals need to breathe in order to live.

Hot-air balloons have hot air inside them. The hot air is lighter than the cold air around the balloon, so the balloon rises into the sky and flies.

Wind is moving air. People use the wind's power to fill the sails of boats and push them along.

MAKE A WINDMILL

Cut slits in a square of thick paper. Make holes in the centre and corners. Fold the corners into the middle and line up the holes. Push a pin through them. Thread on a bead. Push the pin through a plastic drinking straw, a bead and a piece of cork. Blow the windmill to make it spin.

Hang-gliders launch themselves into the air from high places. Then they glide through the sky on currents of warm air called thermals. Thermals rise up into the sky from the land.

A flying lemur cannot really fly. As it jumps from tree to tree, it spreads out flaps of skin between its arms and legs. These help it to glide through the air.

Hot and cold

Heat never stays in one place. It moves around all the time, spreading out from warm places to colder ones. This is why hot things cool down and cold things warm up.

Loose clothes trap a layer of air inside them. People in hot countries often wear loose clothing to keep cool.

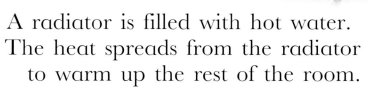

A radiator is filled with hot water. The heat spreads from the radiator to warm up the rest of the room.

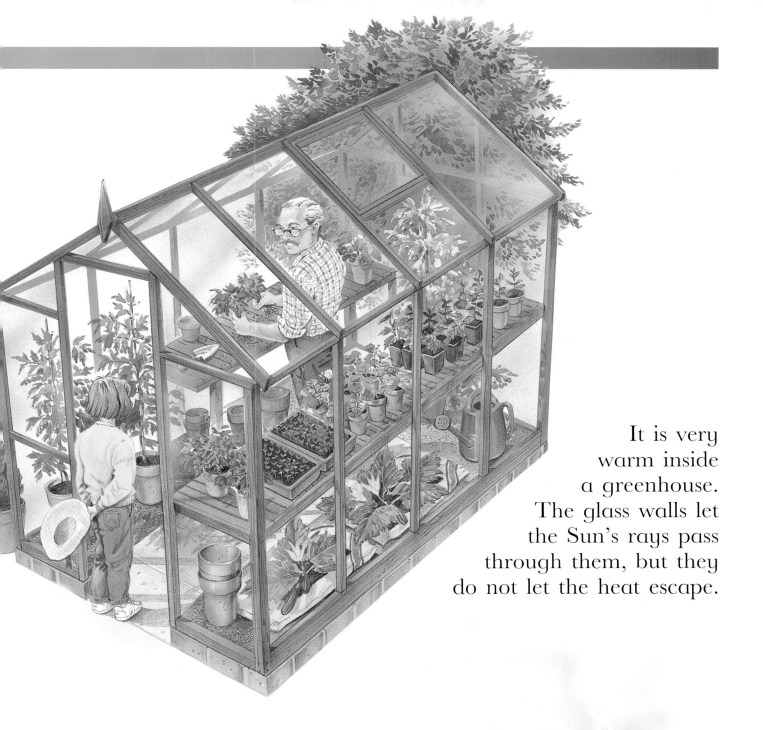

It is very warm inside a greenhouse. The glass walls let the Sun's rays pass through them, but they do not let the heat escape.

The water in this metal saucepan is being heated on a hotplate. The heat passes from the hotplate to the saucepan and then to the water. Metal is used to make saucepans because heat travels through it very easily.

Water

Water is an extraordinary liquid. Sometimes it dries up and just disappears – think of a puddle on a sunny day. At other times drops of water seem to appear from nowhere. Where have they come from?

Ask an adult to boil a cupful of water in a saucepan for five minutes. Let the water cool, then pour it back into the cup. There is less water now. When water boils, some of it turns into an invisible gas called water vapour. This is called evaporation.

When you have a hot shower, some of the water evaporates. As the water vapour cools down, tiny droplets of water form again in the air and you see steam.

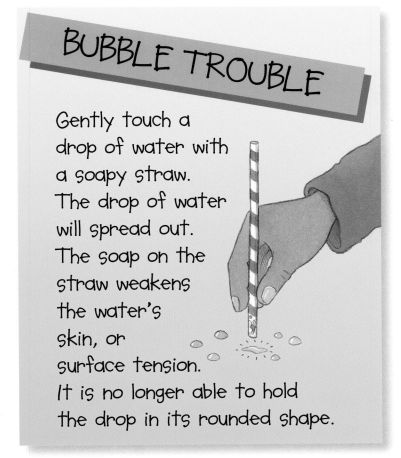

Insects called pond skaters can walk across water without falling in. This is because the surface of water is like a thin, stretchy skin, strong enough to support the weight of an insect. This is called surface tension.

When water vapour hits a cold surface, such as a mirror, it cools down suddenly and turns back into small drops of water again. This is called condensation.

BUBBLE TROUBLE

Gently touch a drop of water with a soapy straw. The drop of water will spread out. The soap on the straw weakens the water's skin, or surface tension. It is no longer able to hold the drop in its rounded shape.

Floating

Some things can float on water. Objects are pulled downwards by their weight, but the water pushes them upwards. If something is light for its size, the water will be able to hold it up and it will float.

Giant icebergs float in the sea because ice is lighter than water. They can even support the weight of polar bears.

Armbands stop you from sinking when you are learning to swim. This is because they are full of air. Air is much lighter than water, so it helps you to float and keeps you safe.

Drop a lump of modelling clay into a bowl of water and it will sink. Make another ball of modelling clay the same size into a boat and it will float. The boat has a much larger surface than the ball of modelling clay. This means it is lighter for its size, so it can float.

Whether or not an object floats depends on its shape and what it is made out of. Objects made of metal or glass don't usually float. Wooden objects float well. If an object is filled with air it will float better.

Light

Without light, we would not be able to see. Most of our light comes from the Sun. It travels through space very fast. Light is made by hot or burning things. Fires, light bulbs and fireworks all make light.

The Moon cannot make its own light. The moonlight we see is really light from the Sun bouncing off the Moon. The Sun gives out light all the time, because it is a giant ball of burning gases.

MAKE SHADOW PUPPETS

Turn off the light in your room and ask a friend to shine a torch onto a wall beside you. Put your hands between the torch and the wall, then hold them in these different positions, to make animal shadows on the wall. Take it in turns to hold the torch and make animal shadows.

Dog

Giraffe

Bird

When light hits a smooth, shiny surface, like this puddle, it bounces back again and you see a reflection.

Light only travels in straight lines. It will not bend around things. If you block a Sun ray, you make a shadow. At midday, the Sun is high in the sky and your shadow is short.

Your shadow is always longer in the early morning or late afternoon.

Colours

Sunlight looks colourless, but in fact it is a mixture of different colours. You see all these colours in a rainbow, as the raindrops split the sunlight.

On a sunny day, you can make a rainbow with a hose. Stand with your back to the Sun and make a fine spray. You will see red orange, yellow, green blue, indigo and violet

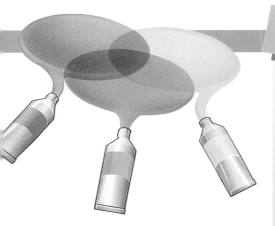

Blue, red and yellow are called primary colours. By mixing them together, you can make most other colours except white.

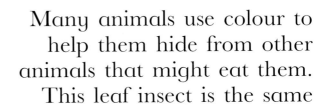

Draw spectacle frames on a piece of thick card. Copy a pair of sunglasses you have at home to make them the right size. Cut the spectacles out and fold back the arms. Tape coloured cellophane sweet wrappers across the eyeholes at the back of the frames. Colour and decorate the frames.

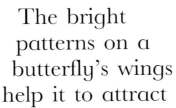

Many animals use colour to help them hide from other animals that might eat them. This leaf insect is the same colour as the leaves it sits on, so it is hard to spot.

The bright patterns on a butterfly's wings help it to attract a mate. The blue eye spots also trick hungry hunters into thinking it is not a butterfly.

301

Time

The clocks and watches we use to tell the time are very accurate. But long ago people could only count the days and nights to measure the passing of time. Later, they invented simple clocks using water or sand to tell the time.

The first number on this watch is the hour. The second number is the minutes. The smaller numbers show the seconds. There are 60 seconds in a minute and 60 minutes in an hour.

An egg timer works like a sand clock. The sand runs from one half of the timer to the other in exactly the time it takes to boil an egg. To start the timer, you turn it upside down to make the sand run into the empty half.

MAKE A WATER CLOCK

Ask an adult to make a hole in the bottom of a plastic pot. Tape a string handle to it. Pin it under an old table. Stand an empty, clear plastic pot under the hanging pot. Pour water into the top pot. After each minute, mark the water level on the bottom pot. You can now use the marks as a clock to measure minutes.

A clock face has 12 numbers on it, one for each hour. The short hand points to the hours. It moves round the clock twice as day because there are 24 hours in a day. The long hand shows how many minutes past the hour it is. It moves around the clock once an hour, or every 60 minutes.

Sounds

There are sounds around us all the time – voices, music, traffic. Every sound you hear is made by something vibrating. This means that it is moving backwards and forwards very quickly.

Sounds move through the air in waves. When someone speaks to you, they make vibrations in the air. The sound waves travel through the air to you. Your ears pick up the vibrations and you hear sounds.

Sounds can also travel through solid things. This boy can hear the girl banging the saucepan through the tabletop.

In a bottle organ, each bottle makes a different sound when you strike it. The more water there is in a bottle, the higher the sound it makes.

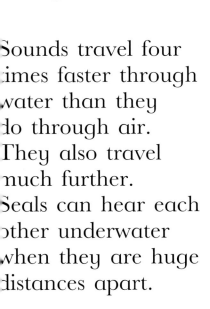

SEEING SOUNDS

You cannot see sound waves, but you can see their effects. Stretch some tin foil tightly over a bowl. Fasten it with an elastic band to make a drum. Put some grains of uncooked rice on the drum, then bang a tin tray next to it. The sound waves will make the rice jump about.

Sounds travel four times faster through water than they do through air. They also travel much further. Seals can hear each other underwater when they are huge distances apart.

Movement

Movement uses up energy, so all moving objects must get the energy that they need from somewhere. There are many different ways that they do this.

Inside a vehicle, there is an engine that burns fuel, such as diesel oil or petrol. When this fuel is burned, it releases energy that the vehicle uses to move.

Surfers use the sea's energy to move. They wait for a big wave, then surf along it as it breaks. They are carried forward by the movement of the water.

You get energy from the food you eat. When you ride a bike, you use up energy stored inside your body. You need to eat regularly so that you do not run out of energy.

Like all animals, these kangaroos get their energy from the food they eat.

You use your own energy to start a toboggan by giving it a push. When it is going downhill the toboggan has enough energy to keep moving by itself.

Weight

The Earth is like a big magnet. It pulls things towards it. This pull is called gravity. It keeps you on the ground and makes the balls you throw into the air come back down again. Gravity also affects how much things weigh.

The pull of gravity makes apples fall from a tree to the ground when they have grown big and heavy.

When you weigh an apple or yourself, the scales are actually measuring the pull of Earth's gravity on the apple and you. The greater the pull of gravity on an object, the more it weighs.

A seesaw is like a balancing scale. It balances when the weight at each end is the same. This seesaw will not move because it weighs more at one end than the other. One of the children is getting off to make the weight even.

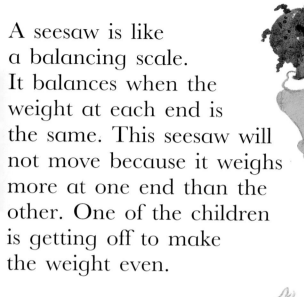

When the children at both ends of the seesaw weigh about the same it is easy to make the seesaw go up and down.

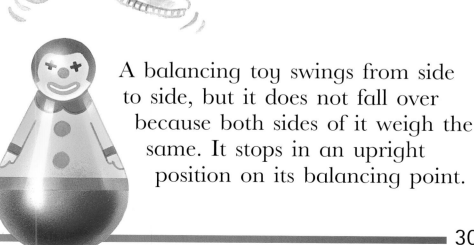

A balancing toy swings from side to side, but it does not fall over because both sides of it weigh the same. It stops in an upright position on its balancing point.

Magnets

Magnets can pull – or attract – things towards them. Materials that are attracted to magnets are called magnetic. Most metals are magnetic, but paper, plastic and wood are not.

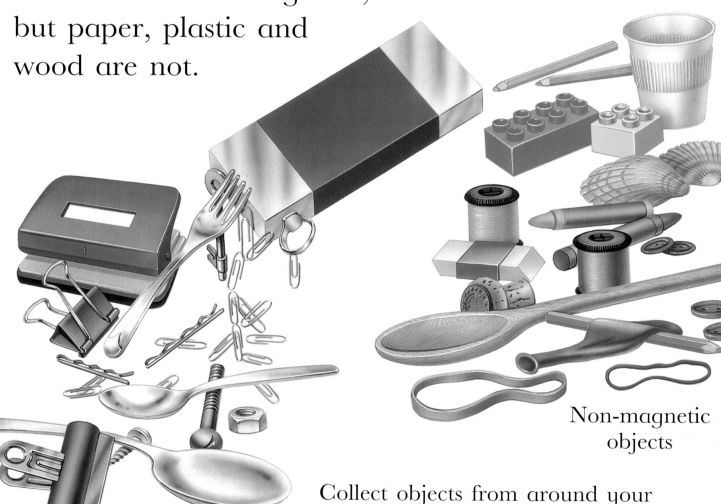

Non-magnetic objects

Magnetic objects

Collect objects from around your home and test them with a magnet to see which materials are magnetic.

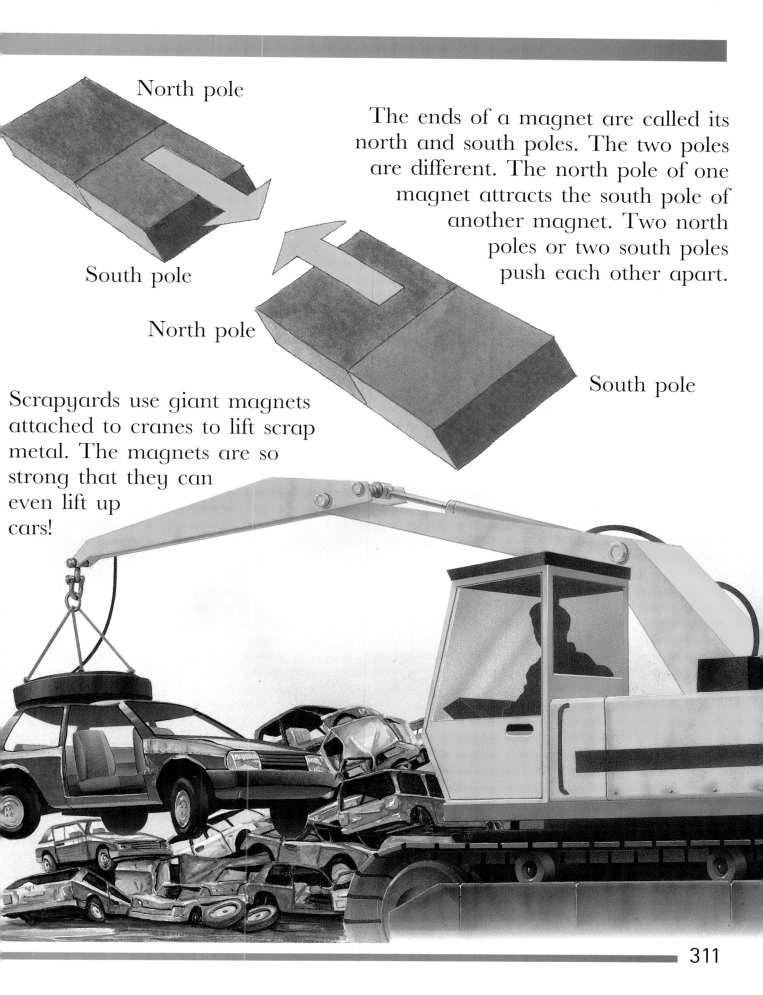

North pole

South pole

North pole

South pole

The ends of a magnet are called its north and south poles. The two poles are different. The north pole of one magnet attracts the south pole of another magnet. Two north poles or two south poles push each other apart.

Scrapyards use giant magnets attached to cranes to lift scrap metal. The magnets are so strong that they can even lift up cars!

Electricity

Electricity can be used to make heat and light and to power all kinds of machinery. It runs through all the wires in your home. Small amounts can also be stored in batteries.

This toaster runs on electricity. You can plug machines into the sockets around your home to make them work. Take care when using electricity – you could get a dangerous electric shock.

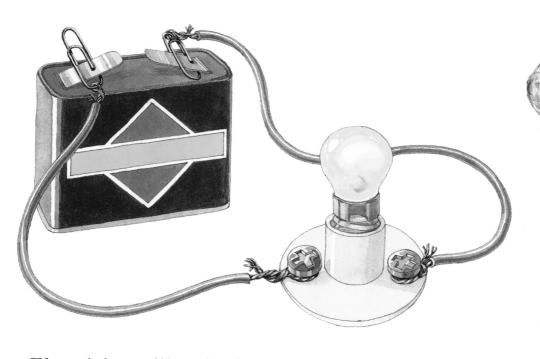

Electricity will only flow along wires if there are no gaps in the circuit. When the lightbulb is connected to the battery like this, the light will switch on.

MAKE A SIMPLE CIRCUIT

Screw a small bulb into a bulb holder. Take two pieces of flex and strip 1 cm of plastic from the ends of each. Attach one end of each piece of flex to a screw of the bulb holder. Attach paper clips to the other ends and clip them to the battery terminals.

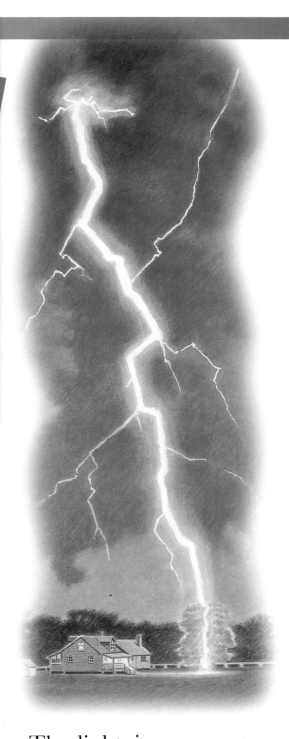

The lightning you see during a thunderstorm is electricity, but it is not the same as the electricity you use at home. Lightning is called static electricity.

Everyday science

Science and new inventions have become part of our everyday lives. Our homes are full of machines that help us to do things more easily. Many things were also made by machines.

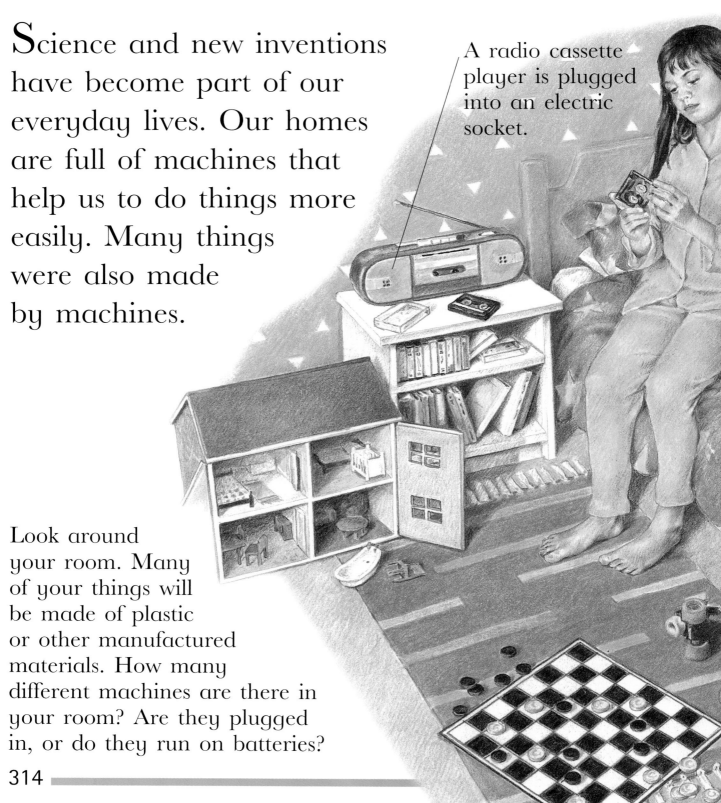

A radio cassette player is plugged into an electric socket.

Look around your room. Many of your things will be made of plastic or other manufactured materials. How many different machines are there in your room? Are they plugged in, or do they run on batteries?

This digital alarm
clock runs on batteries.

You may use
a computer for
your homework,
or to play games.

Trainers are
designed on a
computer and
made by machine.

Index

If you want to read about a subject, you can use this index to find out where it is in the book. It is in alphabetical order.

i

ice 289, 296
ice hockey 252
iguanas 138
illness 222–223
India 192, 238, 241
Indonesia 230, 248, 250
inhalers 223
injections 223
insects 94–95, 111, 124–125,
    158–159, 295, 301
intestines 198
Islam 245
Italy 44, 238

j

Japan 238, 247
Java 250
Jesus Christ 245
jets 279, 280
joints 200–201
Judaism 244
Jupiter 16, 28, 29

k

kangaroos 186, 187
kingfishers 168
koalas 123, 187
Komodo dragons 139
Koran 245

l

lava 44–45
leaves 107, 116
lemurs 291
lichens 118–119

lightning 52, 313
limousines 262
lions 65
lizards 67, 134–135, 138–139
lobsters 157
lorries 260
lungs 198, 208, 209

m

macaws 63
magma 44
magnets 308, 310–311
magnifying glasses 286
mammals 77, 98–99, 176–191
mammoths 101
maps 228–229, 261
maracas 249
marmots 185
Mars 16, 26–27
marshes 58–59
marsupials 186–187
masks 89, 243
meadows 108–109
medicines 193, 222–223, 235
melanin 202
menorah 244
Mercury 16, 20, 35
metal 288, 293, 297, 310–311
metamorphosis 146–147
meteorites 32, 97
meteors 32
mice 122, 185
Milky Way 14
Mongolia 230
monkeys 178–179
Moon 10, 24–25, 298
moons 26, 28, 29, 30, 31
mosques 245
mosses 118–119
moths 160–161
motor cycles 264, 265

mountains 42, 48–49, 56
Muhammad 245
muscles 206–207, 220
Muslims 245
mussels 156

n

Navajo 242
nectar 110, 158
Neptune 17, 30
nerves 203, 204–205
nests 91, 174–175
nettles 127
newts 144
nomads 230
noodles 239
North Pole 68–69
nuts 113

o

oak trees 105
oasis 67
octopus 153
oil rigs 43, 234–235
opossums 187
orang-utans 179
oranges 113
orchids 109, 111
ostriches 167
otters 188
owls 66, 171
oxygen 107, 208–209, 290

p

paddle steamers 274
paddy fields 237
pandas 193
paper 288, 310

Acknowledgments

The publishers would like to thank the following artists for their contributions to this book:

Hemesh Alles, Marion Appleton, Mike Atkinson, Craig Austin, Julian Baker, Julie Banyard, John Barber, Andrew Beckett, Tim Beer, Richard Bonson, Derick Bown, Maggie Brand, Derek Brazell, Peter Bull, John Butler, Martin Camm, Jim Channel, Robin Carter, Adrian Chesterman, Dan Cole, Jeanne Colville, Tom Connell, Joanne Cowne, Peter Dennis, Sandra Doyle, Richard Draper, Brin Edwards, Colin Emberson, Diane Fawcett, James Field, Michael Fisher, Chris Fobey, Chris Forsey, Andrew French, Terence J. Gabbey, Peter Goodfellow, Ruby Green, Ray Grinaway, Terry Hadler, Nick Hawken, Tim Hayward, Karen Hiscock, David Holmes, Steve Holmes, Adam Hook, Christian Hook, Liza Horstman, Biz Hull, Mark Iley, Ian Jackson, Rob Jobson, Kevin Jones, Pete Kelly, Roger Kent, Tony Kenyon, David Kerney, Deborah Kindred, Steve Kirk, Mike Lacey, Stuart Lafford, Terence Lambert, Ruth Lindsay, Bernard Long, Chris Lyon, Kevin Maddison, Alan Male, Adam Marshall, Josephine Martin, David McAllister, Doreen McGuiness, Eva Melhuish, Steve Noon, Chris Orr, Nicki Palin, Darren Pattenden, Bruce Pearson, Liz Pepperell, Jane Pickering, Maurice Pledger, John Potter, Nigel Quigley, Sebastian Quigley, Elizabeth Rice, John Ridyard, John Rignall, Gordon Riley, Bernard Robinson, Eric Robinson, Eric Robson, Mike Roffe, David Russell, Mike Saunders, John Scory, Stephen Seymour, Rob Shone, Guy Smith, Clive Spong, Mark Stewart, Charlotte Stowell, Lucy Su, Treve Tamblin, Myke Taylor, Ian Thompson, Jean Paul Tibbles, Chris Turnball, Richard Ward, Ross Watton, Phil Weare, Rhian West James, Steve Weston, Lynne Willey, Ann Winterbotham, David Woods, Dan Wright, David Wright

Every effort has been made to credit the artists whose work appears in this book. The publishers apologise for any inadvertant omissions. We will be pleased to amend the acknowledgments in any future editions.